LIST OF RECIPES

INTRODUCTION

Eating is one of life's sweet pleasures—so is cooking and serving food to others. And that's what we've been doing at Moosewood since 1973. The Moosewood cuisine is continually evolving. In this recipeasel, we introduce the latest and greatest, the leanest and greenest, and some of the best recipes from Moosewood Restaurant. Our recipes are straightforward and easy to prepare. Over time each dish has been tested and refined so that these recipes should not intimidate a beginning cook and yet will interest the more experienced chef.

More than two decades ago, we were just discovering how to be vegetarians. Soybeans and brown rice were a challenge. Yogurt was a little exotic, remember? Well, since then we've found the world full of foods and flavors to taste and savor. And you know, this vegetarian food is not just loved by vegetarians. Many of us are not strict vegetarians and neither are most of our customers, who come to Moosewood for the good food.

We're excited to be part of the developing American vegetarian cuisine. We think that the real inspiration for our cooking is an openness to ethnic and regional foods—and a readiness to mix and match in the American melting-pot tradition, taking the best and most interesting and throwing it together in new ways to create something unique and wonderful.

Moosewood, the restaurant, has drawn much of its character from the town in which it has grown up. Ithaca, New York, is perhaps the most cosmopolitan little city on the continent. Nestled at the foot of Cayuga Lake between Cornell University and Ithaca College, it more closely resembles a cleaned-up, stripped-down version of Manhattan's Upper West Side than other sleepy towns in the Finger Lakes region. In the late '60s, Ithaca was home to a number of counter-cultural communes; today a network of collectives, cooperatives, and community action groups influences the political and economical climate.

Our restaurant is a worker-owned, democratically-operated business. Management decisions are made by group consensus which at times may seem laborious, but is actually surprisingly effective. Twenty-three years of continuous operation have worked many of the bugs out of the system and several twenty-three-year veterans are still

around to lend their expertise.

Each owner (and that's all 20 of us) is also a worker who may be a cook, waiter, menu planner, or dishwasher. Our salaries are based on an equal wage, and we have a flexible schedule with options to work a variety of jobs or to learn new skills. In addition, there are apprentices and employees who frequently join the collective when there are openings. There's no one boss, much to the wonderment of those who come in asking to see the manager and are shown into the offices of the salad-maker. We're interested in helping each other, so if your waiter's very busy, the cook may serve you dinner.

Now to the recipes: they're organized in an obvious, common-sense way, so that if you have a yen for pasta, you can flip through that section and find something that will satisfy. Follow recipes closely the first time and read them over at least twice before starting. Before you put the recipeasel away, make notes on the meal—you may have wished for a hint of dill to be more dominant, or you might prefer lemon juice to vinegar. That's how we work with our own recipes, which are covered in a thicket of scribbles from the cooks. Then play with the recipe a bit next time—follow your intuitions and whims.

Most of all, taste as you go along. Add a little of a particular ingredient to a small portion before you're generous with it. A good hand with the herbs, spices, and salt and pepper is an acquired skill, and it makes all the difference in the final sparkle of your food.

You'll find a few familiar recipes here—good old guacamole and good old hummus, for instance—but they are requested so often at the restaurant that it was unthinkable to leave them out of this recipeasel. And there are a few at the other extreme; if wasabi, wakame, nori, annato, and tamarind aren't in your kitchen repertoire, check them out in the appendix and give them a try.

At Moosewood, we're always creating new dishes while keeping the old ones alive and well on the main menu. If someone asks what keeps us going, the answer is, first of all, we love food. But also, over the years, we've learned that sharing wonderful food with friends and family is only the tangible reward. It's the care and imagination we give daily to our food that yields a sustaining nourishment for the spirit. If we have a secret, that's it—and it's also why we work gladly. For us, good food and good spirits are inseparable.

SOUPS

ABOUT SOUPS

You can confidently create a good soup with almost anything, with or without a recipe, if you follow certain guidelines and procedures. Begin by sautéing onions and other vegetables in oil or butter. Most dried herbs, such as bay leaf, thyme, oregano, and basil, should be gently sautéed with the vegetables before liquid is added. But the essential oils of fresh herbs and of some dried herbs, such as dill, tarragon, and chervil, are more fragile and may easily be cooked away; add these herbs toward the end of soup making.

Add liquid and simmer the soup until the vegetables are tender. We recommend vegetable stock as the liquid base, although water may be used. Simmer soups gently. Don't boil a soup or you may alter the color and flavor, destroy vitamins and nutrients, and lose the fragrance of the herbs. If you're using milk or tahini, over-heating the soup will make them curdle. Dairy products, such as milk, yogurt, and sour cream, should be added gradually when the soup is off the heat. Any soup should be reheated slowly.

There are several ways to thicken soup. You can mix a roux–a mixture of butter and flour–with some hot stock or milk and blend it into the soup. Cream cheese and sour cream are good ingredients to mellow the flavor and thicken cream soups. You can use leftover cream and cheese sauces as a base for many soups. Or, to avoid butterfat, you can purée a portion of the soup with cooked potatoes and then combine the puréed and chunky parts of the soup for a thick, rich texture.

One of the most obvious and economical rewards for maintaining a whole foods kitchen is that most of the snippings and peelings and unused parts of raw vegetables can be used to make a good stock with little effort. The water left over when vegetables are steamed is not only tasty but full of vitamins. And in many leftovers you have the beginnings of soup. You can use leftover Spicy Peanut Sauce (recipe #90) in Mushroom-Sesame-Tofu Soup (recipe #9) or leftover filling from North Indian Stuffed Eggplant (recipe #49) as a base for Potage St. Cloud (recipe #12).

CHILLED CANTALOUPE-AMARETTO SOUP

SERVES 4 TO 6

This soup is just short of divine ecstasy–but only if the cantaloupe and peaches are in season, fragrant and ripe.

* * *

In a blender, purée small amounts of the fruit with the liquids until all the ingredients are used. The soup should be very smooth. Stir in the nutmeg or cinnamon. Chill several hours before serving.

HERE'S A PLEASANT SUMMER MEAL:

Chilled Cantaloupe-Amaretto Soup

An antipasto platter

Fettuccine with pesto sauce

Crusty Italian bread

A light white wine

- 1 fresh, ripe cantaloupe, peeled, seeded, and cubed
- 2 fresh, ripe peaches, peeled, pitted, and chopped
- 1 teaspoon pure almond extract
- 2 cups heavy cream (or milk or half-and-half)
- ¼ cup amaretto liqueur
- 2 tablespoons fresh lemon juice
- pinch of ground nutmeg or cinnamon *(optional)*

CHILLED SPINACH-YOGURT SOUP

SERVES 4 TO 6

A smooth, green soup with a bright, tart-edged taste.

✵ ✵ ✵

Sauté the onions in the oil on low heat. After about 10 minutes, add the potatoes, salt, pepper, and stock or water. Bring to a boil, then reduce the heat and cover. Simmer until the potatoes are tender, about 10 to 15 minutes. Add the spinach.

When the spinach is wilted but still bright green (2 or 3 minutes), remove from the heat and stir in the milk and dill. Blend in a food processor or blender, in batches, until it is very smooth. Whisk in the yogurt.

Chill for about 4 hours. The soup will thicken as it cools. If it is too thick, whisk in some milk, stock, or water. Adjust the seasoning after it has chilled. Serve garnished with a pinch of nutmeg.

Accompany with Armenian Stuffed Cabbage (recipe #46) or Kolokithopita (recipe #72).

2 tablespoons vegetable oil
1½ cups chopped onions
1 medium potato, chopped
1 teaspoon salt
dash of black pepper
1½ to 2 cups Vegetable Stock (recipe #17) or water
10 ounces spinach, washed and stemmed
2 cups milk
2 to 3 teaspoons chopped fresh dill (1 teaspoon dried)
1 cup plain yogurt

nutmeg, preferably freshly grated

SCANDINAVIAN APPLE SOUP, HOT OR COLD

SERVES 4 TO 6

A simple soup that works for any season—cold in summer, hot in winter. It's particularly good for brunch.

✳   ✳   ✳

Melt the butter in a small skillet and slowly sauté the onions, stirring occasionally, until they are translucent. Meanwhile, core and seed the apples and cut them unpeeled into bite-size chunks. Place the apple chunks in a soup pot with the stock or water and simmer covered on medium heat until the apples are soft, about 15 minutes.

Using a blender or food processor, purée the onions, apples, and stock. Return the mixture to the soup pot and add the spices and cream. The amount of cream used determines the richness of the soup. To serve hot, reheat the soup, keeping it under a boil to avoid curdling. Just before serving, remove the soup from the heat and adjust the sweet-tart ratio with honey and/or lemon juice.

To serve cold, add cream and taste. Adjust sweetness-tartness with honey and/or lemon juice. Chill at least 2 hours.

Ladle the soup, hot or cold, into cups or bowls and top with a spoonful of unsweetened whipped cream and a dusting of ground cinnamon.

Serve for brunch with Mushroom-Leek Frittata (recipe #53) or as a prelude to Mushroom-Tofu-Pecan Stuffed Squash (recipe #51).

2 tablespoons butter
¾ cup chopped onions
10 tart eating or sauce apples, about 3 pounds
3 ½ cups Vegetable Stock (recipe #17) or water
½ teaspoon cinnamon
⅛ teaspoon ground cloves
pinch of nutmeg, preferably freshly grated
1 cup heavy cream or milk
honey (*optional*)
fresh lemon juice (*optional*)
unsweetened heavy cream, whipped
ground cinnamon

MISO BROTH

SERVES 4 TO 6

Miso broth is a staple of Japanese cuisine. Miso Soup is simple and nutritious and is especially satisfying during the depths of winter, when it can warm you from the inside out.

✳ ✳ ✳

Place the wakame in a bowl, cover it with hot water, and set it aside to soak.

Bring the 6 cups of water and the soy sauce to a gentle simmer. Add the carrots, onions, and ginger and simmer covered for several minutes. Drain the wakame, chop it, and add it to the soup. Simmer the broth on low heat for 30 minutes.

Add a small amount of the vegetable broth to the miso and stir it into a paste. Then add the miso paste to the soup, stirring until it is dissolved. Simmer the soup gently just a few minutes longer, taking care that it does not come to a boil.

For variation, try adding broccoli spears, chopped cabbage, sliced mushrooms, tofu, or tofu kan (see Appendix). You may prefer to sauté the vegetables lightly in a spoonful of vegetable oil before adding them to the broth. For a heartier soup, add ½ cup of cooked rice or soba noodles (see Appendix).

Garnish each serving with chopped scallions and toasted sesame seeds and add a few drops of dark sesame oil for its wonderful fragrance.

We consider this soup the perfect prelude to Japanese Braised Eggplant (recipe #48) or Sweet and Sour Vegetables and Tofu (recipe #60).

6 cups water
2 tablespoons tamari soy sauce
1 medium carrot, julienned
1 cup thinly sliced onions
1 teaspoon grated fresh ginger root
2 tablespoons miso (see Appendix)
chopped scallions
toasted sesame seeds
dark sesame oil (see Appendix)
1 5x2-inch strip of wakame (see Appendix)

TOMATO-GARLIC SOUP

SERVES 6

This simple soup can be made in ten minutes and yet it always receives raves. Served with plenty of warm bread and fresh salad, it makes a lovely dinner for unexpected company.

Sauté the garlic in the olive oil very briefly, taking care not to brown it. Stir in the paprika and sauté for another minute, stirring continuously, and taking care that it doesn't scorch. Stir in the tomato juice and heat. Add the wine. Simmer 5 to 10 minutes.

Garnish with croutons, freshly grated Parmesan cheese, and chopped fresh parsley.

VARIATIONS:

· *Mediterranean:* Add cooked garbanzo beans and garnish with shredded feta cheese and chopped fresh parsley.

· *Mexican:* Add Tabasco sauce and garnish with shredded cheddar cheese and tortilla chips.

3 tablespoons olive oil
3 to 6 large garlic cloves, minced or pressed
8 cups tomato juice or undrained canned tomatoes puréed in a blender
1 tablespoon Hungarian sweet paprika (*see Appendix*)
¼ to ½ cup red wine or dry sherry (*optional*)

Croutons
freshly grated Parmesan cheese
chopped fresh parsley

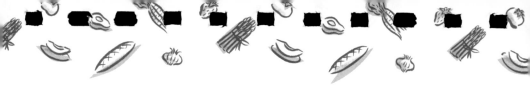

HUNGARIAN VEGETABLE SOUP

Serves 6 to 8

As appropriate for lunch with the kids as for late night suppers. Adding a cup of cooked egg noodles will create an even heartier soup.

In a large soup pot, sauté the onions and garlic in oil until the onions are translucent. Add the paprika, marjoram, carrots, and cabbage and cook on medium heat for 5 minutes. Add the remaining vegetables and salt, reduce the heat, cover, and cook for 5 more minutes. Finally, add the liquids and seasonings and simmer until all the vegetables are tender, about 25 minutes.

Serve with a dollop of sour cream or yogurt and a crusty black bread.

3 tablespoons vegetable oil or butter
2 cups chopped onions
2 garlic cloves, minced or pressed
2 tablespoons Hungarian sweet paprika (*see Appendix*)
½ teaspoon Hungarian hot paprika (*optional*)
¼ teaspoon dried marjoram
2 small carrots, cut into ½-inch rounds
2 cups thinly sliced cabbage
1 cup cut green beans
2 green peppers, chopped
1 small zucchini, cut in half lengthwise and sliced in half-moons
2 cups sliced mushrooms (8 ounces)
2 large tomatoes, chopped
salt to taste
5 cups Vegetable Stock (recipe #17) or water
2 cups tomato juice
½ cup dry red wine
2 tablespoons tamari soy sauce
1 tablespoon dried dill
sour cream or yogurt

YOGURT-BARLEY SOUP

SERVES 4 TO 6

This appealing Middle Eastern soup is a little tart and brightened with fresh mint.

✣ ✣ ✣

Combine the barley and stock or water in a soup pot and bring to a boil. Simmer the barley, covered, while preparing the vegetables in a separate pan.

Sauté the onions in the butter until translucent. Add the carrots and continue to cook, stirring frequently, until the carrots are tender. Add a little water if necessary to prevent the vegetables from sticking.

When the barley is tender, add the vegetables, mint, and seasonings to the soup pot. Simmer for an additional 10 minutes, then stir in the yogurt and parsley. Carefully warm the soup on low heat, adding more stock if it is too thick.

This soup tastes even better the next day, but reheat it gently, or the yogurt will curdle. As the barley cooks and later as it cools, it releases starch which thickens the soup. If the soup becomes too thick, add more stock or water to thin it.

Yogurt Barley Soup works well as part of a Middle Eastern-style array of foods—olives, tomatoes, hard-boiled eggs, and pita with spreads.

⅔ cup uncooked barley*
5 cups Vegetable Stock (recipe #17) or water

2 tablespoons butter
2 cups chopped onions
1 medium carrot, diced
1 tablespoon chopped fresh mint (½ teaspoon dried)
1 ½ teaspoons salt
black pepper to taste
2 cups plain yogurt
2 tablespoons minced fresh parsley

*2 ½ cups of cooked barley and 3 cups of stock or water may be substituted for the uncooked barley.

RECIPEASEL #7

PISTOU

SERVES 4

Pistou is the French word for pesto. This soup is a must for pesto lovers and stone soup aficionados.

✤ ✤ ✤

Sauté the onions and carrots in olive oil for 3 or 4 minutes. Add the green peppers, potatoes, and string beans and sauté for another 4 minutes. Add the zucchini and stock or water, cover, and bring to a boil. Add the navy beans and lower the heat.

Simmer the soup for about 15 minutes or until the vegetables are tender but not overcooked. Stir in the pesto. Add salt and pepper to taste.

Try this soup with pasta and a light sauce such as Ramatuelle (recipe #74). This meal can be appropriately topped off with Wine-Poached Pears (recipe #112) and your best Maurice Chevalier imitation.

2 tablespoons olive oil
¾ cup diced onions
1 medium carrot, sliced
1 small green pepper, chopped
1 medium potato, diced
1 ½ cups cut string beans
1 cup sliced zucchini
4 cups Vegetable Stock (recipe #17) or water
1 cup cooked, drained navy beans (*see Appendix*)
½ to ¾ cup Winter Pesto (recipe #77)
salt and black pepper to taste

MUSHROOM-SESAME-TOFU SOUP

SERVES 6

A classic of eclectic post-hippie cuisine, this chunky protein-rich soup is a complete meal with bread and a crisp salad. This is one of our favorite soups (and dairyless, to boot!).

Sauté the onions and ginger in the oil for 4 minutes. Add the celery and continue to sauté for about 5 minutes. Stir in the mushrooms, cover, and cook on low heat for about 10 minutes. Stir in the cayenne, salt, and bay leaves. Add the tomatoes, their juice, and the stock or water.

Simmer covered for about 20 minutes. Add the tahini and peanut butter, stirring briskly to dissolve. Finally, add the cubes of tofu. Continue to simmer on very low heat for 20 minutes, stirring occasionally to prevent scorching.

2 tablespoons peanut oil or vegetable oil
1 ½ cups chopped onions
1 teaspoon grated fresh ginger root
3 celery stalks, sliced
2 cups sliced mushrooms (8 ounces)
⅛ teaspoon cayenne
½ teaspoon salt
2 or 3 bay leaves
4 cups undrained whole tomatoes, chopped
1 cup Vegetable Stock (recipe #17) or water
2 tablespoons tahini (*see Appendix*)
3 tablespoons peanut butter
1 cake of tofu, pressed (*see Appendix*) and cut into ¾-inch cubes

ARMENIAN LENTIL SOUP

SERVES 6

Most lentil soups are healthful, but can be a little boring. This one is healthful and exotic. The addition of aromatic herbs, spices, and–surprise!–apricots transform a homey classic into something excitingly eccentric.

✤   ✤   ✤

Rinse the lentils, and then bring them to a boil in the stock or water. Reduce the heat and simmer covered for 20 minutes. Add the chopped apricots and simmer covered for another 20 minutes.

Meanwhile, sauté the onions in the oil until translucent, then add the eggplant and 4 or 5 tablespoons of water. Cook covered on medium heat, stirring occasionally, until the eggplant is almost tender. Add the remaining vegetables, dried spices, and salt. Cover and cook until tender, about 10 minutes.

Stir the sautéed vegetables into the cooked lentil-apricot mixture and simmer for 15 minutes. Add the parsley and mint and serve.

Armenian Lentil Soup is perfect with dark bread, sharp cheese, and a crisp salad.

1½ cups dried lentils
6 cups Vegetable Stock (recipe #17) or water
½ cup chopped dried apricots (4 ounces)

3 to 4 tablespoons vegetable oil
1 cup chopped onions
2 to 3 cups cubed eggplant
1½ cups chopped tomatoes, fresh or canned
1 green pepper, chopped
¼ teaspoon cinnamon
¼ teaspoon ground allspice (or another ¼ teaspoon cinnamon, if preferred)
¼ teaspoon cayenne or crushed red pepper
1 tablespoon paprika
1½ teaspoons salt
3 tablespoons chopped fresh parsley
1 tablespoon chopped fresh mint

EGG-LEMON SOUP WITH SPINACH

SERVES 6

Inspired by the classic Greek avgolemono soup, our variation includes spinach and garbanzo beans for added color, nutrition, and taste.

✤ ✤ ✤

In a soup pot, sauté the onions and garlic in oil until the onions are translucent, about 10 minutes. Add the carrots, dill, and 4 cups of the stock or water, cover, and bring to a boil. Reduce to a simmer and cook until the carrots are tender, about 10 minutes. While the carrots are cooking, whisk together the eggs, lemon juice, and remaining one cup of liquid.

Remove the pot from the heat and whisk in the egg mixture. Then reheat gently, stirring continuously, until the egg mixture thickens. Do not allow the soup to boil or it will curdle. Stir in the rice, spinach, and garbanzo beans and season to taste with salt and pepper.

When the soup is hot, serve at once. The spinach should still be bright green, contrasting nicely with the bits of orange carrot.

We suggest serving with Zucchini-Feta Casserole (recipe #56) or as a lovely first course for Fish à la Grecque (recipe #82).

2 tablespoons vegetable oil
2 cups finely chopped onions
1 large garlic clove, minced or pressed
2 medium carrots, finely chopped
½ teaspoon dried dill
5 cups Vegetable Stock (recipe #17) or water
3 eggs
4 tablespoons fresh lemon juice
1 cup cooked brown rice (*see Appendix*)
1½ cups stemmed and chopped fresh spinach
½ cup cooked garbanzo beans (*see Appendix*)
salt and black pepper to taste

POTAGE ST. CLOUD

SERVES 6 TO 8

A vivid chartreuse-colored soup. The sweet pea potage provides a perfect backdrop for the light curry.

✤ ✤ ✤

Sauté the onions and garlic in butter until golden. Add the potatoes, parsnips, carrots, turmeric, curry powder, and stock or water and simmer until the vegetables are tender, about 20 minutes. Reserve 1 cup of the peas for garnish and add the rest to the pot. Cook frozen peas for 10 minutes, fresh ones for 5 minutes. In a blender or food processor, purée the hot soup with the half-and-half until very smooth. Add salt and pepper to taste. Cook the reserved peas until just tender to garnish individual servings.

Leftover filling from North Indian Stuffed Eggplant (recipe #49) is the perfect "scratch" from which to start this soup (replacing the first eight ingredients). Purée the filling in a blender or food processor with the peas and hot stock or water and the half-and-half. Finish the soup as directed.

Serve with Corn Bread (recipe #109) and Artichoke Heart and Tomato Salad (recipe #22).

3 tablespoons butter
1½ cups chopped onions
1 garlic clove, minced or pressed
3 medium potatoes, sliced
1 medium parsnip, sliced (*optional*)
1 large carrot, sliced
2 teaspoons turmeric
½ to 1 tablespoon curry powder (*see Appendix*)
5 cups Vegetable Stock (recipe #17) or water
6 cups green peas, fresh or frozen
2 cups half-and-half or milk
salt and black pepper to taste

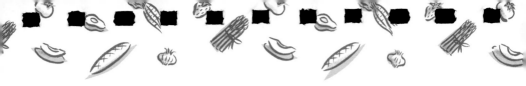

POTAGE À LA BRETONNE

SERVES 6

A comforting, homey soup from Brittany.

✤ ✤ ✤

Cook the beans in water to cover (adding more water as needed) until they are tender.

Sauté the garlic, leeks, and onions in the butter until the onions are translucent. Add the herbs and seasonings and continue to sauté for 5 to 10 minutes more, until the onions begin to brown. Add the tomatoes and half of the lemon juice and simmer covered for 10 minutes. Stir in the beans and their juice and cook for another 10 minutes on low heat. Stir occasionally to prevent sticking. Remove the bay leaves.

Purée the soup in a blender or food processor adding the cream and stock or water as you blend. Stir in the remaining lemon juice. Add more stock or water if the soup needs to be thinned. Adjust the seasonings. Gently reheat on very low heat.

We like to serve this soup with French Rice Salad (recipe #18) and a wedge of Brie.

1¼ cups navy beans, soaked (see Appendix)

¼ cup butter
2 garlic cloves, pressed or minced
3 leek bulbs (white parts only), well rinsed (see Appendix) and thinly sliced
2 cups diced onions
2 bay leaves
¾ teaspoon dried thyme
¾ teaspoon salt
⅛ teaspoon black pepper
3 medium tomatoes, chopped
⅓ cup fresh lemon juice
1 cup heavy cream or half-and-half
3 to 4 cups Vegetable Stock (recipe #17), bean stock, or water

CREAMY SQUASH SOUP

Serves 4 to 6

A lovely, slightly sweet soup, the essence of autumn. This soup can become a non-dairy one by using oil or margarine instead of butter, and apple juice instead of cream.

✢ ✢ ✢

Clean the squash, cut it in half, and scoop out the seeds. Place it, cut side down, on a lightly oiled baking pan, cover, and bake at 350 degrees about one hour, until soft. Butternut squash may be peeled, cubed, and boiled rather than baked, if you prefer, but baking is easiest and heightens the flavor.

Meanwhile sauté the onions in the butter until they are translucent. Add the carrots, potatoes, apples, and water. Bring the vegetables to a boil, lower the heat, and simmer about 20 minutes, until all the vegetables are tender.

When the baked squash has cooled, scoop out the soft insides and discard the skins. Combine the squash, vegetables, and stock with the milk, cream, or apple juice in a blender or food processor and purée in several batches to a smooth, creamy consistency.

Heat the soup on low heat until it is hot, but not boiling. Add the cinnamon. Season to taste with salt and black pepper.

Serve this soup with a hearty dark bread and a soufflé. If you have baked squash left over, you might use it in Squash Rolls (recipe #107).

1 acorn squash or small buttercup or butternut squash (about 2 cups cooked)
3 tablespoons butter, vegetable oil, or margarine
2 cups chopped onions
1 small carrot, diced
1 medium potato, diced
2 cooking apples, peeled, cored, and chopped
3½ cups water
1½ cups milk or apple juice or 1 cup heavy cream
⅛ teaspoon cinnamon
salt and black pepper to taste

POTAGE JACQUELINE

SERVES 4 TO 6

A soothing soup, gently seasoned to emphasize the innate goodness of sweet potatoes. This recipe was created by our own Jacqueline Lisa Wichman.

✤ ✤ ✤

Melt the butter in a heavy saucepan and sauté the onions until translucent, stirring occasionally. Add the celery and ginger and continue to cook until the onions begin to brown. Add the sweet potatoes, water, bay leaf, and salt and pepper and bring to a rapid boil. Reduce the heat, cover, and simmer 15 to 20 minutes, until the sweet potatoes are tender.

Remove and discard the bay leaf. Purée the soup mixture with the milk and heavy cream in small batches in a blender or food processor. Adjust the salt and pepper to taste and reheat gently. Take care not to boil the soup.

Garnish Potage Jacqueline by floating a thin lemon round on each serving.

2 tablespoons butter
2 cups chopped onions
1 celery stalk, chopped
1 teaspoon grated fresh
   ginger root
3 medium sweet potatoes,
   peeled and thinly sliced
4 cups water
1 bay leaf
½ teaspoon salt
black pepper to taste
1 cup milk
½ cup heavy cream

CRÈME ANDALOUSE

Serves 6

Leeks, tarragon, and cream add a French touch to this sophisticated version of a Spanish soup.

✤ ✤ ✤

Sauté the leeks in the butter until soft. Add the tomatoes and simmer for 10 minutes. Add the remaining ingredients, except the lemon juice and cream. Simmer until the potatoes are thoroughly cooked.

Purée the cooked vegetables in a blender, adding the lemon juice and cream. Gently reheat, taking care not to boil which could cause it to curdle.

Garnish with croutons and parsley. This pretty pastel soup is nicely accompanied by Salat Tangiers (recipe #19) or Mushroom Pâté (recipe #41) and crackers.

2 tablespoons butter
3 leek bulbs (white part only), rinsed (see Appendix) and chopped
6 fresh tomatoes, chopped, or 4 cups undrained canned tomatoes
7 cups Vegetable Stock (recipe #17) or water
4 medium potatoes, cubed
1 teaspoon salt
½ teaspoon dried tarragon
⅛ to ¼ teaspoon cayenne
1 teaspoon fresh lemon juice
½ cup heavy cream
herbed croutons (see Appendix)
¼ cup chopped fresh parsley

VEGETABLE STOCK

YIELDS 2 QUARTS

Vegetable Stock is a broth made by simmering vegetables in water until they are soft and their flavors and nutrients have been released into the liquid. Then the stock is poured through a strainer and the vegetables are either discarded or used, puréed, to thicken a soup.

The best vegetables to use in stock are carrots, peeled onions, celery, zucchini, potatoes, parsley, parsnips, sweet potatoes, and squash. We often throw in chunks of apples or pears to sweeten the stock a little. It's wise to avoid the strongly flavored vegetables of the cabbage family, such as broccoli and cauliflower, and turnips, rutabagas, and kohlrabi–and vegetables with bleeding colors, such as beets, red cabbage, and greens (unless you intend to make a borscht or cream of green soup). Green peppers and eggplant will make the stock bitter. Be cautious about adding lots of tomatoes or other acidic fruits or vegetables to the stock, which may curdle a soup containing dairy products. Wash all vegetables (especially root) thoroughly.

�֍ �֍ �֍

Put all of the ingredients into a large pot, bring to a boil, and simmer for 45 minutes to an hour. Strain and use.

For spicier stock throw in some garlic cloves, skins and all, and a small amount of tomato. For a specifically Asian broth, add ginger, scallions, and shiitake mushrooms (*see Appendix*). Or, make it sweet for a carrot purée or Scandinavian fruit soup with the addition of sweet potato or winter squash.

2 large unpeeled potatoes, quartered
2 large carrots, peeled and sliced thickly
1 large onion, peeled and quartered
1 celery stalk, chopped
1 apple or pear, seeded and quartered
1 bay leaf
12 peppercorns
10 cups water (2½ quarts)

SALADS

FRENCH RICE SALAD

Serves 6

Here's a creative way of dealing with leftover rice–the result is a cool and crunchy, multicolored dish. It keeps well, tasting even better the next day, and it's easy to eat when you're on the road. The marinade in this recipe has many other uses as well. Try using it to marinate steamed artichokes or asparagus.

✢ ✢ ✢

Place the cooked rice in a large bowl. Steam the carrots, peppers, mushrooms, and peas separately until tender but still firm. Add the steamed vegetables, celery, and parsley to the rice. Whisk the marinade ingredients together. Pour the marinade over the vegetable-rice mixture and toss gently.

Refrigerate until well chilled, stirring occasionally, so the marinade will flavor the rice. When ready to serve, garnish with tomato wedges and green olives.

Other serving options and accompaniments:

·A sprinkle of freshly grated Parmesan or feta cheese on the top

·Add dried currants, toasted pine nuts, or almonds

·A wedge of Brie, fontina, Jarlsberg, or any other good flavorful cheese

·Steamed and marinated vegetables

·Stuff a tomato shell or green pepper half with rice salad and bake it for a wintertime lunch

3 cups cooked rice (*see Appendix*)
1 cup diced carrots
1 cup diced green or red bell peppers
1 cup sliced mushrooms (4 ounces)
1 cup green peas, fresh or frozen
1 small celery stalk, finely chopped
2 tablespoons chopped fresh parsley

Marinade
¼ cup olive oil
¼ cup vegetable oil
¼ to ⅓ cup fresh lemon juice
1 garlic clove, pressed
one or two of these herbs:
    1 tablespoon fresh or 1 teaspoon dried tarragon, basil, dill, marjoram

tomato wedges and green olives

SALAT TANGIERS

SERVES 4 TO 6, MORE IF USED AS A SIDE DISH

A confetti-like Moroccan pastiche of colors and flavors.

✤ ✤ ✤

Put the couscous, salt, and saffron, if you're using it, in a large bowl, and stir in the boiling water. Cover and let sit for 10 to 15 minutes, stirring occasionally to fluff.

Meanwhile, steam the carrots, green peppers, and beans separately. As soon as each vegetable is barely tender, add it to the couscous. Stir in the red onions, currants, and almonds.

Whisk together the marinade ingredients, leaving out the mint if you used saffron in the couscous. Toss the couscous and vegetable mixture with the marinade and chill at least an hour to allow the flavors to marry.

Serve with Baba Ganouj (recipe #37) or Tzatziki (recipe #98) for a light lunch or with Armenian Lentil Soup (recipe #10) to create a perfect protein.

1½ cups dry couscous
½ teaspoon salt
pinch of saffron (*optional*)
1¼ cups boiling water
1 cup diced carrots
1 large pepper, diced
1 cup cut green or wax beans
⅓ cup finely chopped sliced red onions
⅓ cup currants
½ cup almonds, toasted and chopped

MARINADE
½ cup vegetable oil
4 tablespoons fresh lemon juice
½ teaspoon salt, or more to taste
¼ teaspoon cinnamon
3 tablespoons orange juice (or apple cider)
4 tablespoons chopped fresh parsley
1 tablespoon fresh spearmint (1 teaspoon dried)
pinch of cayenne

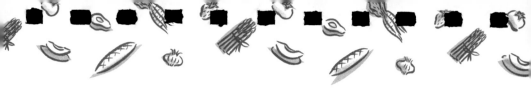

TUSCAN POTATO SALAD

SERVES 8

The addition of the creamy ricotta cheese and robust Parmesan cheese makes this an unusual potato salad. Substantial enough for a salad-dinner, it's a fine side dish as well.

✢ ✢ ✢

Cook the potatoes in boiling salted water until just tender. Drain the potatoes. While they are still hot, stir in the rest of the ingredients. Tuscan Potato Salad can be served warm but improves with chilling.

Garnish with parsley just before serving.

Tuscan Potato Salad is well complemented by Tomato-Garlic Soup (recipe #5).

3 pounds (about 12 cups) peeled, cubed red or new white potatoes
⅔ cup freshly grated Parmesan cheese (2 ounces)
1 cup ricotta cheese (9 ounces)
4 garlic cloves, pressed
½ red onion, very thinly sliced
½ cup olive oil
6 tablespoons cider vinegar
salt and black pepper to taste

½ cup chopped fresh parsley

MIDDLE EASTERN CARROT SALAD

SERVES 4 TO 6

An easy, light, and refreshing salad, sparkling with lemon and mint. Maple syrup gives it an interesting twist.

* * *

Mix all the ingredients together and chill at least one hour before serving.

In the summertime, when we serve our customers on the patio, we frequently offer a colorful Middle Eastern salad plate: a cup of Chilled Spinach-Yogurt Soup (recipe #2), a square of Kolokithopita (recipe #72), and side dishes of Tzatziki (recipe #98), a marinated artichoke half, and Middle Eastern Carrot Salad.

- 4 cups grated carrots
- 3 tablespoons fresh lemon juice
- 3 tablespoons vegetable oil
- ½ teaspoon ground coriander seeds
- ¼ teaspoon salt
- 2 teaspoons chopped fresh mint (½ teaspoon dried)
- 1 tablespoon chopped fresh parsley
- 1 to 2 teaspoons honey, sugar, or maple syrup *(optional)*

ARTICHOKE HEART AND TOMATO SALAD

SERVES 4

Artichoke hearts are one of the few canned foods that we recommend and do use in our kitchen. Here they are combined with fresh, ripe tomatoes in a light marinade.

Cut each tomato into 6 wedges and each artichoke heart into halves. Blend the rest of the ingredients, pour over the vegetables, and toss. Chill for 20 minutes.

Serve on a bed of greens with fish or a cheese-filled strudel, such as Kolokithopita (recipe #72). Or fill a pita with Artichoke Heart and Tomato Salad, greens, and grated feta or Parmesan cheese.

4 ripe, medium tomatoes
8 canned artichoke hearts (not marinated)

½ cup vegetable oil
⅛ cup wine vinegar or white vinegar
1 garlic clove, pressed
1 tablespoon fresh tarragon (¼ teaspoon dried)
1 tablespoon fresh basil (¼ teaspoon dried)
salt and black pepper to taste

PEPPERS AND CAPERS

SERVES 4 TO 6

We use Peppers and Capers as an interesting salad served on lettuce, as a sharp and assertive side dish, as a garnish for tossed salad, as a topping for baked fish, and as a stuffing for a pita bread with greens and feta or Parmesan cheese.

✳ ✳ ✳

Heat the oil in a large, heavy skillet until quite hot. Fry the pepper strips. It is best to do this in two batches, turning the peppers often for even and thorough cooking. They should be well fried–even a little browning doesn't hurt. Drain the peppers on paper towels to absorb as much excess oil as possible.

Place the fried peppers, red onions, and capers in a bowl and dress them with the olive oil, vinegar, garlic, and salt. Toss well and chill.

½ cup vegetable oil
5 or 6 large green and/or red peppers, sliced in long, wide strips
1 tablespoon capers (*see Appendix*)
1 small red onion, thinly sliced
2 tablespoons olive oil
2 tablespoons red wine vinegar
1 garlic clove, pressed or minced
salt to taste

PASTA PRIMAVERA

SERVES 6 TO 8

This is one of our favorite pasta salads. Make it in the winter using frozen basil or pesto.

✤ ✤ ✤

Cook the pasta al dente (*see About Pastas*). Drain it and rinse with cold water. Sauté the garlic in olive oil for 1 minute. Add the mushrooms and cook on medium heat until just tender. Remove from the heat. Steam the asparagus and peas until tender.

Toss all the vegetables with the pasta. Add the rest of the ingredients and toss well.

Serve at room temperature on lettuce, with extra Parmesan.

1 pound pasta (shells or short tubes)
2 tablespoons olive oil
3 garlic cloves, minced
3 cups sliced mushrooms (12 ounces)
2 cups asparagus, cut into 1-inch pieces
1 cup green peas
5 medium tomatoes, chopped
3 tablespoons chopped fresh basil and 1 table-spoon olive oil
2 tablespoons fresh lemon juice
½ cup freshly grated Parmesan cheese (1½ ounces)
½ cup chopped fresh parsley
½ cup thinly sliced sun-dried tomatoes (*optional*)
salt and black pepper to taste

GOI GA-VIETNAMESE SALAD

SERVES 4 TO 6

This is a dish for people who enjoy hot and spicy food. Different elements of the salad are prepared separately and assembled on the serving table. It's a salad that is a meal in itself, a spirited blend of ingredients with added visual appeal.

* * *

Cook the rice, place in a bowl, and set aside. Prepare the vegetables, toss them together in a bowl, and set aside. Mix together the sauce ingredients in a bowl. Put the peanuts and the mung bean sprouts in bowls.

To serve the salad, simply take everything to the table. Pass the bowls. On individual plates each person will pile salad vegetables on rice, pour on some sauce, and top with peanuts and sprouts.

1 cup cooked rice (*see Appendix*) per serving

½ small red onion, very thinly sliced
1 medium carrot, cut into thin strips
1 green pepper, cut into thin strips
10 ounces fresh spinach, cleaned, stemmed, and dried
1 small cucumber, peeled, cut in half lengthwise, seeded, and sliced diagonally
other raw vegetables, such as turnips and white radishes, cut into thin strips
some leafy lettuces (buttercrunch, ruby, Boston, curly), torn into bite-size pieces

VIETNAMESE SAUCE
3 tablespoons white vinegar
3 tablespoons Thai or

(more)

Today far too many restaurants serve tiny, over-decorated portions of exotic food in an atmosphere of expansive pretentiousness. Moosewood remains untouched by this trend. It is famous all through the Finger Lakes region for its inventive combination of fresh local ingredients, generous helpings, and friendly, casual ambience.

–Alison Lurie
author of *Foreign Affairs*

other Asian fish sauce (*see Appendix*)*
2 small dried hot peppers, soaked in ½ cup boiling water until soft and then minced
2 tablespoons fresh lemon juice

2 cups unsalted roasted peanuts, coarsely chopped
1 cup mung bean sprouts

*For a vegetarian version of this sauce, substitute tamari soy sauce for the Asian fish sauce.

SPICY SZECHUAN NOODLES

SERVES 4 TO 6

Some years ago, Ashley Miller and Bob Love, both Moosewood cooks, introduced this popular dish to the rest of us. They had discovered it in Chinese cooking classes with Stella Fessler, one of our Ithaca mentors. We've been grateful for it ever since.

Today, similar spicy noodle salads seem to be on the menus of most Asian restaurants and every slightly trendy café but it is still a favorite with us, and we think you'll be glad to learn how easy it is to make at home.

✢　✢　✢

Cook the pasta al dente in salted water. Drain it and rinse with cold water. Mix the peanut butter, warm water, soy sauce, vinegar, and oils. Toss the noodles with the bean sprouts, cucumber, and sauce. Top with chopped scallions and/or toasted sesame seeds, if desired. This dish is most flavorful served at room temperature.

Spicy Szechuan Noodles are attractive served on crisp leaves of romaine. Create an Asian ensemble with Broccoli-Mushroom-Tofu Salad (recipe #27) or Asian Asparagus Salad (recipe #28).

½ pound whole wheat spaghetti or soba noodles (*see Appendix*)

¼ cup peanut butter (or a mixture of peanut butter and tahini)
¼ cup warm water
3 tablespoons tamari soy sauce
2 tablespoons wine vinegar (preferably rice wine vinegar)
1 tablespoon dark sesame oil (*see Appendix*)
1 teaspoon hot chili oil (*see Appendix*)
2 cups fresh mung bean sprouts
1 cucumber, peeled, cut lengthwise, seeded, and cut into crescent slices

chopped scallions
toasted sesame seeds

BROCCOLI-MUSHROOM-TOFU SALAD

SERVES 6

A salad of contrasting tastes and textures: crisp-tender broccoli, mushrooms, and smooth tofu in a ginger marinade.

* * *

Press the tofu while preparing the vegetables.

Rinse the broccoli. Discard the woody bottoms of the stems. Cut off the florets on 1-inch stems. Peel the thick lower stalks, cut them into lengthwise strips, and then again, diagonally, into 1-inch pieces. Steam the broccoli until just tender and still bright green. Rinse immediately with cold water (to stop the cooking and preserve crispness) and drain.

Steam the sliced mushrooms briefly, a minute or two. Rinse with cold water and drain. Combine the broccoli, mushrooms, and scallions in a large bowl.

In a small bowl whisk together the marinade ingredients. Pour half the marinade over the vegetables. Pour the rest of the marinade over the cubed tofu in a separate bowl. Allow to marinate for an hour or more, gently turning the vegetables and the tofu several times with a wooden spoon.

Toss everything together just before serving.

This salad goes well with Spicy Szechuan Noodles (recipe #26) or brown rice tossed with toasted sesame seeds. We often serve it on a bed of salad greens, topped with toasted walnuts or almonds, and garnished with a wedge of cantaloupe.

3 cakes of tofu, pressed (*see Appendix*) and cubed
1 large bunch of broccoli
3 cups sliced mushrooms (12 ounces)
4 scallions, sliced diagonally

MARINADE
3 garlic cloves, pressed
1 tablespoon grated fresh ginger root
3 tablespoons dark sesame oil (*see Appendix*)
6 tablespoons tamari soy sauce
6 tablespoons Chinese rice wine (*see Appendix*) or dry sherry
¼ teaspoon ground fennel seeds
⅛ teaspoon cayenne

ASIAN ASPARAGUS SALAD

SERVES 4 TO 6

W hen you hear the first spring peepers and the breeze feels gentle, celebrate the end of winter with asparagus prepared in an Asian way that is as elegant in its simplicity as a spring haiku. Sometimes boiled green vegetables lose their color, even when you are careful not to overcook them. Follow our directions for keeping those greens green. Broccoli and green beans are also delicious with this marinade.

✤ ✤ ✤

Whisk together the marinade ingredients and set aside.

Wash the asparagus and remove the tough ends. Ease the asparagus spears into boiling water to cover. The water will stop boiling with the addition of the asparagus. Keep covered on high heat until the water returns to a rapid boil. Cook one or two minutes longer, until the asparagus are tender but still crisp. Plunge the cooked asparagus immediately into cold water to stop the cooking and set the color. Drain well, place in shallow bowl, and cover with the marinade. Chill at least 30 minutes, but do not wait longer than 2 hours before serving.

Garnish with a sprinkle of toasted sesame seeds.

This dish is also very good served hot. Just drain the hot, cooked vegetables, toss them with the marinade, garnish, and serve.

Asian Asparagus Salad is well paired with Spicy Szechuan Noodles (recipe #26).

1½ pounds fresh asparagus

MARINADE
2 tablespoons tamari soy sauce
1½ teaspoons sugar
1 tablespoon dark sesame oil (see Appendix)
1 tablespoon white vinegar
1 tablespoon Chinese rice wine (see Appendix) or dry sherry
½ teaspoon grated fresh ginger root
½ teaspoon Chinese chili paste (optional), (see Appendix)

lightly toasted sesame seeds

L.D.'S CREAMY GREEN DRESSING

Yields 2 cups

This is one of our most frequently requested and admired recipes–our daily house dressing. L.D. (Linda Dickinson) has been working at Moosewood since 1973 and so has had plenty of time to perfect this recipe.

Blend all of the ingredients, except the buttermilk, for one minute. While the blender is running, slowly pour in the buttermilk. As soon as the dressing thickens, turn off the blender or the dressing will separate and become runny. It should be thick and creamy. Chill at least 30 minutes so the flavors have a chance to meld.

Other herbs can be used to vary this dressing. Dill, tarragon, oregano, a dab of Dijon mustard, and freshly ground black pepper are all possible additions or substitutions. Fresh herbs in season are always our choice when available. Yogurt or sour cream may be substituted for the buttermilk. However, buttermilk makes the most creamy and stable (non-separating) dressing.

Refrigerated and tightly covered, it will stay fresh for up to a week. If the dressing separates, reblend.

1 cup vegetable oil
2 tablespoons cider vinegar or fresh lemon juice
1 teaspoon honey or 2 tablespoons apple juice
5 or 6 spinach leaves
2 tablespoons chopped fresh parsley
1 teaspoon fresh basil (¼ teaspoon dried)
1 teaspoon fresh marjoram (¼ teaspoon dried)
½ teaspoon salt
1 garlic clove, pressed
1 cup buttermilk

VINAIGRETTE SALAD DRESSING

YIELDS 1¼ CUPS

This dressing will enhance, without upstaging, a wide variety of salads. Create a basic vinaigrette by omitting the herbs or choose just one or two as a more dominant note. This will keep indefinitely if refrigerated.

❊   ❊   ❊

Whisk together all ingredients.

½ cup vegetable oil
¼ cup olive oil
⅓ cup cider vinegar or red wine vinegar
2 garlic cloves, pressed
¼ teaspoon salt
1 tablespoon Dijon mustard
⅛ teaspoon black pepper
1 tablespoon chopped fresh parsley
2 tablespoons chopped fresh basil, marjoram, dill, chives, tarragon in any combination (2 teaspoons dried)

YOGURT-TAHINI DRESSING

YIELDS 2 CUPS

A quick dressing, popular in Middle Eastern countries, Yogurt-Tahini has its own distinctive tang and fullness.

* * *

In a medium bowl, whisk together all ingredients until smoothly blended. If the dressing is thicker than you like, add more milk or water.

This dressing is versatile. It's good with salads, pitas, Tofu Burgers (recipe #71), Soyfalafel (recipe #70), or dipping vegetables.

Refrigerated and tightly covered, it will keep for up to a week.

¾ cup plain yogurt
⅓ cup tahini (*see Appendix*)
3 to 6 tablespoons fresh lemon juice
2 garlic cloves, pressed
½ teaspoon salt
¼ cup milk or water
pinch of ground cumin (*optional*)
1 tablespoon chopped fresh parsley (*optional*)

BLUE CHEESE DRESSING

YIELDS A GENEROUS 2½ CUPS

A lusty dressing for ardent lovers of blue (no matter how you spell it) cheese.

✤ ✤ ✤

Put all the ingredients except a third of the blue cheese in a blender or food processor. Blend to a smooth, creamy consistency. Crumble the remaining blue cheese and stir it into the dressing.

Refrigerated and tightly covered, Blue Cheese Dressing will stay fresh for 4 or 5 days. Try it as a dip, as well as on salads.

1 garlic clove, minced or pressed
6 ounces blue cheese
1½ cups sour cream
½ teaspoon salt
¼ teaspoon black pepper
2 tablespoons fresh lemon juice
½ cup milk

MISO-GINGER DRESSING

YIELDS 2½ CUPS

A very popular and lively non-dairy dressing which has introduced many of our customers to the use of miso as a delicious, nutritious seasoning. Perfect on a fresh spinach salad with grated carrot. Excellent as a marinade for steamed broccoli and tofu.

✢ ✢ ✢

In a blender on low speed, combine 3 tablespoons miso, the ginger, vinegar or lemon juice, and sesame oil. Gradually add the vegetable oil in a thin, steady stream until thoroughly mixed. Then very slowly add the water until the dressing is thick and creamy. Taste. If a richer flavor is preferred, blend in an additional tablespoon of miso.

Miso-Ginger Dressing will keep almost forever stored in the refrigerator. If the dressing separates, reblend.

3 to 4 tablespoons light miso (*see Appendix*)
2 tablespoons grated fresh ginger root
¼ cup cider vinegar or ⅓ cup fresh lemon juice
2 tablespoons dark sesame oil (*see Appendix*)
1 cup vegetable oil
½ cup water

TAHINI-GARLIC DRESSING

YIELDS 1½ CUPS

A robust garlic dressing with a nutty, sesame taste. This strongly flavored dressing is at its best on a very simple salad of one lettuce, such as romaine or buttercrunch.

✳ ✳ ✳

Place all the ingredients in a blender or food processor and blend thoroughly.

Refrigerated, this dressing will keep indefinitely.

½ cup tahini (*see Appendix*)
2 tablespoons vegetable oil
¼ cups fresh lemon juice
½ cup water
1 teaspoon cider vinegar
2 teaspoons tamari soy sauce
1 or 2 garlic cloves, pressed
⅛ teaspoon black pepper

SANDWICHES
AND DIPS

TEMPEH REUBEN

Get out the dill pickles! This is one of our favorite sandwiches at Moosewood. When it is on the lunch menu, the workers have to be chased out of the kitchen to ensure that there will be enough for the customers.

✤ ✤ ✤

Sauté the onions and garlic in oil for 2 or 3 minutes until the onions begin to soften. Add the tempeh and continue to sauté on low heat, stirring frequently, for about 20 minutes. While the tempeh is browning, get the remaining ingredients ready. When the tempeh is crisp and lightly browned, add the soy sauce.

Build the sandwiches on the toast by layering the tempeh mixture, Russian dressing, sauerkraut, and Swiss cheese. Broil the sandwiches until the cheese is melted. Serve piping hot.

¼ cup vegetable oil
2 cups chopped onions
2 garlic cloves, minced or pressed
8 ounces tempeh (*see Appendix*), thinly sliced or cubed
2 teaspoons tamari soy sauce

4 slices bread, preferably rye, toasted
1½ cups Russian dressing
1½ cups sauerkraut, warmed
1½ to 2 cups grated Swiss cheese (5 to 7 ounces)

MEXICAN VEGETABLES ON CORN BREAD

SERVES 4 TO 6

This is a filling open-faced sandwich to be eaten with a fork for a casual, hearty lunch. Wash it down with lemonade or a beer.

✤ ✤ ✤

In a large skillet, sauté the onions and garlic in the oil for 5 minutes. Add the carrots, cover the pan, and sauté for another 5 minutes, stirring occasionally. Stir in the remaining vegetables and seasonings and cook on low heat until the vegetables are just tender. The mixture should be saucy; add more tomato juice if necessary.

Serve over hot Corn Bread and top with sour cream or cheese. For a hearty variation, try adding some sautéed tempeh cubes.

2 tablespoons vegetable oil
2 cups chopped onions
2 garlic cloves, minced
3 carrots, cut into half-moons
1 medium zucchini, cut into half-moons
1 green pepper, diced
2 cups corn, fresh or frozen
2 cups undrained canned tomatoes, chopped
1 teaspoon ground cumin
1 teaspoon ground coriander
1 tablespoon chopped fresh cilantro (*optional*)
salt and cayenne to taste
additional tomato juice, if needed

CORN BREAD (recipe #109)
1 cup sour cream or 1 cup grated Monterey Jack or cheddar cheese (3 ounces)

BABA GANOUJ
(Middle Eastern Eggplant Purée)

YIELDS 3 CUPS; SERVES 4 TO 6 AS A SANDWICH SPREAD AND MORE AS A DIP

The tantalizing taste and texture of roasted eggplant is eternally appealing.

✤ ✤ ✤

Pierce the skins of the eggplants several times with a fork and place them on a baking sheet. Bake the whole eggplants at 400 degrees until they are crinkly on the outside and very soft inside, about 40 minutes to 1 hour, depending on their size. Or, for an authentically smoky flavor, skewer the whole eggplants and roast them directly over a flame until they are well charred on the outside. In either case, when the eggplants are cool enough to handle, scoop out the insides. Purée the eggplant pulp and the remaining ingredients in a food processor until smooth. Or mash the eggplant with a fork until smooth and then stir in the remaining ingredients. Cool to room temperature.

Top with chopped scallions and a little olive oil and serve as a dip for raw vegetables with toasted pita bread on the side. Decorate with cherry tomatoes and Greek olives.

2 pounds eggplant, preferably thin, small ones if roasting over a flame
6 tablespoons fresh lemon juice
4 tablespoons tahini (*see Appendix*)
1 to 4 garlic cloves, pressed or minced
2 tablespoons finely chopped fresh parsley
salt to taste
chopped scallions
olive oil

HUMMUS WITH TAHINI

SERVES 6 TO 8 AS A SANDWICH SPREAD OR ENOUGH DIP FOR A PARTY

Hummus is an authentic staple food of Middle Eastern cuisine. It's a perfect balance: the mild and nutty flavor of garbanzo beans is enhanced by zesty lemon and robust garlic.

* * *

- 3 cups well-cooked garbanzo beans (*see Appendix*)
- 1 cup garbanzo bean cooking liquid or water
- 4 to 5 tablespoons fresh lemon juice
- ½ cup tahini (*see Appendix*)
- 3 garlic cloves, pressed
- 1 teaspoon salt
- ⅛ teaspoon cayenne (*optional*)
- ¼ cup chopped fresh parsley

Hummus is most easily made in a food processor. However, a blender or even a potato masher may be used if the garbanzo beans are very tender.

If using a food processor, process the garbanzo beans with ½ cup of the bean liquid and the lemon juice. Then add the tahini, garlic, and seasonings, being careful not to overblend. The texture of hummus should be both rough and creamy at the same time. Add as much of the reserved cup of liquid as you need to get the consistency you want. Stir in the chopped parsley.

If using a blender, the hummus should be made in 2 or 3 batches with frequent stops to stir the contents up from the bottom of the blender using as much of the reserved bean liquid or water as needed.

If done by hand, mash the garbanzo beans with a bit of their liquid in a flat-bottomed bowl with a potato masher or large pestle. Add the rest of the ingredients and mix well.

Serves as a dip with raw vegetable sticks or toasted pita bread. This is also a fine side dish with a Mediterranean menu.

Hummus will keep for several days refrigerated. It freezes very well.

MEDITERRANEAN EGGPLANT CAVIAR

Serves 4 to 6

Moosewood's Wynelle Stein has vivid memories from her childhood of many chilly, drizzling Philadelphia days made warm and sunny as her mother and grandmother prepared this special dish to conjure up the old country.

✤ ✤ ✤

Preheat oven to 400 degrees. Pierce the skins of the eggplants several times with a fork. Place the whole peppers and the eggplants right on the oven rack and line the bottom of the oven with aluminum foil to catch any juices. Done this way, the eggplants and peppers will roast evenly without being turned.

While the eggplants and peppers are roasting, combine everything else in a large bowl.

When the peppers blister in about 25 minutes, remove them from the oven and cool for 5 minutes. Then peel, seed, and chop the peppers and add them to the bowl. The eggplants will take about 50 minutes. Remove them from the oven, scoop out the pulp, chop it finely, and add it to the bowl. Discard the eggplant skins. Add salt and cayenne to taste.

Marinate the "caviar" in the refrigerator for at least 2 hours before serving, or better yet overnight.

This eggplant salad is great with Greek olives, crackers, crudités, and pita bread and harmonizes well with other Middle Eastern appetizers, such as Hummus with Tahini (recipe #38) and Tzatziki (recipe #98).

2 medium eggplants
2 peppers (1 red and 1 green is nice)

1 celery stalk, finely chopped
1 large tomato, chopped
1 tablespoon capers, chopped
2 tablespoons chopped fresh parsley
2 tablespoons olive oil
2½ teaspoons cider or wine vinegar
2 garlic cloves, pressed
salt and cayenne to taste

GUACAMOLE

YIELDS AT LEAST 2 CUPS

It's difficult to improve upon the taste of fresh, ripe avocado. Mixed with a bit of garlic and lemon juice, you've got the makings of a dip, appetizer, or sandwich filling.

* * *

Slice the avocados in half. Remove the pit and scoop out the avocado flesh with a spoon. If you're using smooth, green-skinned large Florida avocados, which are less rich than the smaller, bumpy, darker-skinned California avocados, you may wish to add a teaspoon of vegetable oil.

In a food processor or a mixing bowl, combine the avocado, garlic, and lemon or lime juice to taste. Stir in salt and red pepper to taste. Serve immediately or chill covered. After chilling, taste again for lemon juice.

2 ripe avocados
1 to 3 garlic cloves, pressed
fresh lemon or lime juice
to taste
salt and red pepper to taste

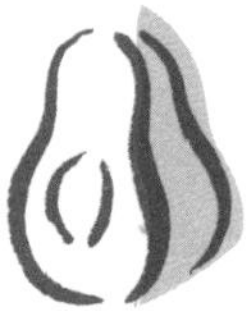

MUSHROOM PÂTÉ

SERVES 6

The Vegetarian Epicure by Anna Thomas is one of our favorite cookbooks. Her mushroom pâté inspired us to develop this recipe. Mushroom Pâté can be served as a snack, appetizer, side dish, or picnic fare.

✢ ✢ ✢

Sauté the scallions and celery in the oil until the scallion whites are translucent. Add the mushrooms, basil, and thyme and continue to cook on low heat until the mushrooms have softened.

Combine the sautéed vegetables with the rest of the ingredients and blend in a food processor or, in small quantities, in a blender.

Oil a medium loaf pan and line it with waxed paper, allowing several inches of waxed paper to hang over the sides of the pan. Oil the waxed paper. Spoon in the pâté. Fold the waxed paper across the top and bake for about 1½ hours at 400 degrees. The pâté is done when a toothpick inserted in the center comes out clean.

When the pâté is cool, fold back the waxed paper on top. Invert the pâté onto a platter and carefully peel away the paper.

Arrange thin slices of the pâté with greens on a platter and serve with various breads, crackers, dips, and crudités for an opulent display.

1 tablespoon vegetable oil
⅔ cup chopped scallions
1 celery stalk, chopped
5 cups sliced mushrooms (1 pound, 4 ounces)
½ teaspoon dried basil
¼ teaspoon dried thyme

1 cup whole wheat bread crumbs
½ cup walnuts, chopped
¼ cup tahini (*see Appendix*)
2 tablespoons tamari soy sauce
1 cake of tofu, blanched (*see Appendix*) and crumbled
⅛ teaspoon black pepper
⅛ teaspoon cayenne

MAIN DISHES

BUDDHA'S JEWELS

SERVES 4 TO 6

Joan Adler is a longtime Moosewood member. In her continuing quest for the new and exotic menu feature, Joan discovered this delicious, healthful dish. Golden tofu dumplings filled with crunchy bits of vegetable and topped with a shimmering, pungent sauce. As an appetizer this recipe will serve 8 to 10 people.

✳ ✳ ✳

In a large bowl, mix together all the ingredients for the tofu dumplings. Shape into approximately 2 dozen 2-inch balls and place on an oiled baking sheet. Bake at 375 degrees for 45 minutes, until golden and firm.

Combine all the sauce ingredients except the cornstarch in a stainless steel or enamel saucepan. Bring to a boil. Stir in the dissolved cornstarch and simmer, stirring continuously, until the sauce is clear and thickened.

Pour the sauce over the dumplings and serve immediately. Serve Buddha's Jewels with rice and steamed vegetables.

DUMPLINGS
- 3 cakes of tofu pressed and mashed (*see Appendix*)
- 2 tablespoons peanut butter
- 3 tablespoons tamari soy sauce
- 8 scallions, chopped
- 1 green pepper, diced
- 1½ cups chopped mushrooms (6 ounces)
- ¼ cup chopped fresh parsley
- ½ cup diced water chestnuts

SAUCE
- 1½ cups pineapple, orange, and/or apple juice
- ¼ cup maple syrup, honey, or brown sugar
- ⅓ to ½ cup cider vinegar
- ¼ cup tamari soy sauce
- 1 garlic clove, minced or pressed
- 2 tablespoons cornstarch dissolved in 2 tablespoons cold water

SARA'S PIROSHKI
(Potato-Cabbage-Cheese Turnover)

YIELDS 6 LARGE PASTRIES

Traditional piroshki are bite-sized savory pastries. As developed by Sara Robbins they are large, entrée-sized turnovers, which are always very popular at Moosewood. The ingredients are inexpensive and preparation is not difficult. The pastry is simply a rich pie dough.

✳   ✳   ✳

Mix the flour and salt thoroughly. Cut in the butter with knives or a pastry cutter until the mixture resembles coarse cornmeal. Using a fork and as few strokes as possible, mix in the ice water until the mixture can be formed into a ball. Chill the dough for 15 minutes.

Boil the potatoes until tender, then drain and mash them in a large bowl. Sauté the cabbage and onions in butter in a covered skillet until tender, about 15 minutes. Add them to the potatoes and stir in all the remaining ingredients.

Preheat oven to 400 degrees.

Divide the dough into six equal balls. Roll each ball into a thin circle, approximately 6 inches in diameter. Place two or three heaping tablespoons of the filling in the center of each circle, brush the edges with the beaten egg mixture, and fold over to form a half-moon. Press the edges with your fingers or a fork to seal. Carefully lift each piroshki with a spatula and place it on an oiled baking sheet. Brush the top of each pastry with the egg-water mixture and sprinkle with seeds. Bake for

Pastry Dough
- 1½ cups unbleached white flour
- ¼ teaspoon salt
- ¼ pound butter
- 3 to 5 tablespoons ice water

Filling
- 2 cups sliced potatoes
- 3 tablespoons butter
- 2 cups finely chopped cabbage
- 1 cup finely chopped onions
- 1 cup cottage cheese
- 1 cup grated sharp cheddar cheese (3 ounces)
- 1 egg
- ½ teaspoon salt
- 2 tablespoons chopped fresh dill (2 teaspoons dried)
- 2 tablespoons chopped fresh parsley
- 2 tablespoons chopped fresh chives or scallions
- ¼ teaspoon ground caraway seeds

(more)

25 to 35 minutes or until golden brown.

Top with sour cream and serve with Sweet and Sour Red Cabbage (recipe #99) and applesauce.

When we learned Isaac Bashevis Singer was coming to dinner, our resident Yiddish grammarian, Allan Warshawsky, translated the evening's menu into Yiddish. Allan was not originally scheduled to work, but put in a guest appearance in order to wait on the Nobel Prize-winning author.

¼ teaspoon white pepper (or black pepper)

1 egg, beaten with 1 tablespoon water
sesame seeds or poppy seeds for topping (*optional*)

1 cup sour cream

BURRITOS

SERVES 4 TO 6

These savory little packages are a hearty and spicy pairing of a popular, perfect protein combination: beans and corn.

❊ ❊ ❊

Drain the cooked beans and reserve the liquid.

Sauté the garlic and onions in oil for several minutes until the onions are translucent. Add the peppers and all of the spices and continue to sauté until the peppers are tender, stirring occasionally. Cover the vegetables, remove them from the heat, and set them aside.

Mash the beans with a potato masher or wooden pestle and add enough reserved bean liquid to obtain the consistency of stiff mashed potatoes. Mix the mashed beans, sautéed vegetables, corn, olives, and cheese. Salt to taste.

Preheat the oven to 400 degrees.

Place each tortilla flat on the counter. Spoon ½ to ¾ cup of the bean mixture onto the half of the tortilla closest to you. Roll the tortillas from the bottom up, putting pressure on the filling so that it will be evenly distributed and will reach the open edges of the rolled tortilla. Place the burritos, rolled edge down, in an oiled baking pan. Brush them with oil, cover with a damp cotton cloth, and bake, tightly covered with foil, for 45 minutes. Uncover the pan, remove the cloth, and serve immediately, or sprinkle the burritos with the additional grated cheese if desired, and bake about 5 minutes more.

Serve the burritos on heated plates. Top with sour cream.

5 cups cooked pinto or kidney beans (see Appendix)
¼ cup vegetable oil
4 to 5 garlic cloves, minced
4 cups chopped onions
3 medium green peppers, chopped
1½ tablespoons ground cumin
¼ teaspoon cayenne, or to taste (optional)
1 tablespoon ground coriander seeds

1 cup corn
½ cup chopped black olives
1⅓ cups grated sharp cheddar cheese (4 ounces)
salt to taste

12 wheat tortillas
vegetable oil

1 cup grated cheddar cheese (3 ounces) (optional)
1 cup sour cream

STUFFED ZUCCHINI BRETONNE

SERVE 4 TO 6

Flavorful and aromatic. Don't spare the garlic–if sautéed gently, it gives a pungent accent to the dish. This is one of many recipes developed by Allan Warshawsky.

✳   ✳   ✳

Sauté the onions in the olive oil for 5 minutes. Stir in the carrots, celery, salt, pepper, tarragon, dill, and bay leaves and sauté another 5 minutes. Stir in the green peppers and simmer covered until the vegetables are tender. Discard the bay leaves.

Sauté the garlic in the butter, taking care not to burn it. In a blender or food processor, purée 1 cup of the cooked beans with ½ cup liquid.

In a large bowl, gently stir the cream cheese cubes, lemon juice, and red pepper sauce into the sautéed vegetables. Stir in the sautéed garlic and the puréed and whole beans. Taste the filling and adjust the seasonings.

Slice the zucchini in half lengthwise. Carefully scoop out the middle of each zucchini half without breaking the skin. Spoon the filling into each zucchini boat and pack the little boats into a baking pan, propping them against each other and the sides of the pan, so they won't capsize. Add half an inch of water to the bottom of the pan, cover tightly, and bake at 350 degrees for 45 minutes.

Top with chopped parsley.

3 cups cooked and drained navy beans (*see Appendix*)
½ cup liquid from cooking the beans or Vegetable Stock (recipe #17) or water

2 tablespoons olive oil
2 cups chopped onions
1 cup diced carrots
2 celery stalks, diced
½ teaspoon salt
pinch of black pepper
1½ teaspoons dried tarragon
1 teaspoon dried dill
2 bay leaves
1 green pepper, diced

2 tablespoons butter
3 garlic cloves, minced or pressed
4 ounces cream cheese, cubed
1 teaspoon fresh lemon juice
¼ teaspoon hot red pepper sauce

4 medium or 6 small zucchini

chopped fresh parsley

ARMENIAN STUFFED CABBAGE

SERVES 6

Drawing from her Armenian heritage, Laura Branca created this vegetarian version of a classic favorite rich with nuts, aromatic mint, and tangy lemon.

❋ ❋ ❋

Sauté the rice in a tablespoon of olive oil, stirring continuously, for 3 to 4 minutes. The rice will begin to smell "nutty," somewhat reminiscent of popcorn. Add the bay leaves, salt, tomato paste, and water and stir until the tomato paste is dissolved. Cover and cook until tender (*see Appendix*).

Immerse the cored head of cabbage in boiling water. After several minutes, as each leaf begins to separate from the head, gently but nimbly pull it completely off the cabbage and set aside to cool. Continue until there are 12 good leaves to stuff.

Combine the nuts, mint, and parsley in a mixing bowl. When the rice is ready, remove the bay leaves and add the rice to the nuts. Mix in 2 to 3 tablespoons of olive oil, the garlic, and half the lemon juice.

Make a thin sauce by crushing the tomatoes in their juice and then mixing in the salt and pepper, lemon juice, and the remaining olive oil. Thin the sauce with water if necessary. Ladle some of the sauce into a large skillet or soup pot.

Put ⅓ to ½ cup of the rice-nut filling on the thick end of

2 cups uncooked brown rice
1 tablespoon olive oil
2 bay leaves
½ teaspoon salt
1 tablespoon tomato paste
3½ cups water

1 large green cabbage*
1 cup walnuts, finely chopped
1 cup almonds, finely chopped
¼ cup chopped fresh spearmint (1 tablespoon dried)
½ cup chopped fresh parsley
⅓ cup olive oil
3 garlic cloves, pressed or minced
⅓ cup fresh lemon juice
3 cups canned tomatoes
salt and black pepper to taste

yogurt
chopped fresh parsley

each cabbage leaf. Fold the sides over the mixture and then roll up toward the thin edge of the leaf. Arrange the cabbage rolls on top of the sauce, seam side down. Pour the rest of the sauce over the rolls, cover, and simmer for 30 to 45 minutes. Test the cabbage for tenderness by piercing with a fork.

Top with a dollop of yogurt and more chopped parsley if desired. Serve with steamed, fresh green beans and julienned carrots.

*Suzie Tuch, a cousin of Moosewood's Allan Warshawsky, has stuffed many a cabbage leaf in her day and gave us this very useful tip. Freeze a head of cabbage a few days before you intend to make stuffed cabbage. Thaw it the day before and the cabbage leaves will easily peel off the head. Blanch the leaves for a few minutes in boiling water. This is a lot easier than the boil-and-retrieve method of peeling cabbage leaves.

EGGPLANT PROVENÇALE

SERVES 6

Saffron provides the distinctive flavor, color, and ambiance in this Mediterranean stuffed eggplant. The pilaf filling could also be used to stuff zucchini, peppers, or tomatoes, or as an accompaniment to fish.

* * *

Cook the rice (*see Appendix*), sautéing it in olive oil and crumbling the saffron into the pan before adding the water and salt.

Brush a large baking pan with olive oil. Leaving the stems on, slice the eggplants in half lengthwise and place them in the pan, cut side down. Add ¼ cup water and ¼ cup sherry. Cover tightly with aluminum foil and bake at 375 degrees until tender, about 45 minutes.

Meanwhile, sauté the onions in 2 tablespoons olive oil for 10 minutes. Add the peppers, 1 tablespoon sherry, and the cayenne. Sauté covered for 5 minutes. Stir in the tomatoes, currants, parsley, and pepper. Simmer covered a few minutes, until the vegetables begin to release their juices.

Combine the rice and the vegetable mixture.

When the baked eggplants are cool enough to handle, turn them over in the baking pan and gently mash and push to the side the soft middle. Mound the rice pilaf on each eggplant half. Pour ½ cup of tomato juice or water into the baking pan. Cover the pan tightly and return it to the oven to bake about 30 minutes.

Serve garnished with slivered almonds and parsley.

1½ cups uncooked brown rice
1 tablespoon olive oil
generous pinch of saffron
3 cups water
1½ teaspoons salt

2 tablespoons olive oil
3 medium eggplants
¼ cup water
¼ cup sherry

2 tablespoons olive oil
3 cups minced onions
1 large red or green pepper, minced
1 tablespoon sherry
½ teaspoon cayenne (*optional*)
2 medium tomatoes, chopped
½ cup dried currants
½ cup chopped fresh parsley
¼ teaspoon black pepper

½ cup tomato juice or water
½ cup toasted, slivered almonds
chopped fresh parsley

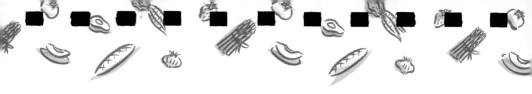

JAPANESE BRAISED EGGPLANT

SERVES 4

Eggplants braised in a Japanese manner in a sweetened sherry sauce are then stuffed with a rich, eclectic filling.

✣ ✣ ✣

Leaving the stems on, cut the eggplants in half lengthwise. Mix together the sherry, soy sauce, and molasses. Oil a baking pan. Pour the sherry mixture into the pan, place the eggplant halves, cut side down, in the pan, cover it tightly, and bake at 350 degrees for 45 minutes, until tender.

Brown the cubed tempeh, ½ cup of the onions, 1 teaspoon of the fennel, and ¼ teaspoon cayenne in oil for 20 minutes, stirring frequently. In a separate pan, sauté the remaining 2 cups onions, the coriander, and the remaining teaspoon of fennel until the onions are translucent. Add the peppers and the mushrooms and sauté another 15 to 20 minutes.

With a slotted spoon, lift the tempeh and onions from the oil. Stir them into the sautéed vegetables. Stir in the tomato paste and 2 tablespoons of the braising liquid. Salt the filling to taste.

Turn the eggplant halves over in the baking pan. With a fork or spoon, carefully mash the pulp and push to the sides, making a hollow in each half without breaking the skins. Fill each hollow with one-fourth of the filling. Cover pan tightly and bake at 350 degrees for 20 minutes.

Serve on a bed of rice, drizzle pan juices over the eggplant. Sprinkle with chopped scallions and toasted sesame seeds.

2 medium eggplants
½ cup dry sherry
⅓ cup tamari soy sauce
1 tablespoon molasses

¼ cup vegetable oil
8 ounces tempeh (*see Appendix*), cubed
2½ cups chopped onions
2 teaspoons ground fennel seeds
¼ teaspoon cayenne
1 teaspoon ground coriander seeds
1 medium green pepper, diced
4 cups sliced mushrooms (1 pound)
3 tablespoons tomato paste
salt to taste

brown rice
chopped scallions
toasted sesame seeds

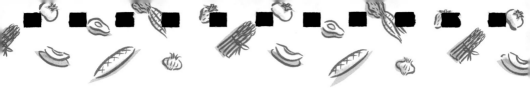

NORTH INDIAN STUFFED EGGPLANT

SERVES 4

If you're a fan of Indian food and would like to prepare something other than a curry, try this creamy yet spicy dish.

✢   ✢   ✢

Leaving the stems on, slice the eggplants in half lengthwise and place cut side down on an oiled baking sheet. Cover and bake at 375 degrees until tender, about 30 to 40 minutes.

While the eggplant is baking, boil the potatoes until tender and then drain. Mash the drained, hot potatoes with the cream cheese in a large bowl. Meanwhile, sauté the onions and the dried spices in oil for 1 minute, then add the ginger and garlic and continue to sauté until the onions are translucent. Add the carrots and cook 5 minutes. Add the peppers and peas and cook until just tender. Stir in the tomatoes and lemon juice. Combine the sautéed vegetables and the potato-cream cheese mixture.

Turn baked eggplant halves over in the baking pan. With a fork or spoon mash the pulp, taking care not to break the skin. Push aside some of the pulp, making a hollow in each half. Mound a quarter of the filling in each. Sprinkle the top with sesame seeds, if desired, and bake covered at 375 degrees for 15 minutes, then uncovered for an additional 15 to 20 minutes.

If you have more filling than needed for the eggplants, try stuffing a green pepper or tomato, too. This is also the perfect leftover to use as a base for Potage St. Cloud (recipe #12).

2 medium eggplants

4 cups cubed potatoes
8 ounces cream cheese, at room temperature

2 tablespoons vegetable oil
2 cups chopped onions
2 teaspoons ground cumin
1 tablespoon ground coriander
1 teaspoon turmeric
½ teaspoon hot red pepper (or 2 small fresh hot peppers, minced)
¼ teaspoon ground cloves
1 tablespoon minced fresh ginger root
2 garlic cloves, minced or pressed
2 medium carrots, diced
1 large green pepper, diced
1 cup green peas, fresh or frozen
1 tomato, diced (*optional*)
2 tablespoons fresh lemon juice

sesame seeds (*optional*)

MEXICAN BEAN STUFFED PEPPERS

S<small>ERVES</small> 4 <small>TO</small> 6

A piquant filling for peppers that features the high protein and appealing texture of tempeh. If you have trouble finding tempeh, use an additional cup of cooked beans in its place.

✳   ✳   ✳

In a heavy skillet, cook the onions and garlic in the oil until they begin to soften. Add the tempeh and sauté, stirring often, until it is browned. Add the tomatoes, corn, and seasonings. Cook covered until thoroughly heated. Mix in the cooked beans, olives, and soy sauce. Adjust the salt and pepper to taste.

Cut the peppers in half lengthwise and remove the seeds. Leave the stems on if you can, because then the pepper halves will hold their shape better during baking. Fill each pepper half with vegetable-tempeh mixture and place in an oiled pan with ½ inch of tomato juice or water in the bottom. Bake tightly covered at 375 degrees for 30 to 40 minutes.

Serve on a bed of rice. Garnish with sour cream or grated cheese.

4 tablespoons vegetable oil
2 cups chopped onions
4 garlic cloves, minced or pressed
8 ounces tempeh (*see Appendix*), in ½-inch cubes
3 tomatoes, chopped
2 cups corn
1 teaspoon ground cumin
2 teaspoons ground coriander seeds
3 cups cooked kidney or pinto beans (*see Appendix*), slightly mashed
½ cup chopped Spanish olives (*optional*)
2 tablespoons tamari soy sauce
salt and black pepper to taste

6 red or green peppers
¾ to 1 cup tomato juice or water
1 cup sour cream or grated cheddar or Monterey Jack cheese

MUSHROOM-TOFU-PECAN STUFFED SQUASH

SERVES 6 TO 8

This is a festive and hearty dish, appropriate for a holiday dinner. It is a perfect Thanksgiving alternative to turkey, served with steamed Brussels sprouts and cranberry sauce, naturally.

✤　✤　✤

Place the squash halves, cut side down, in an oiled baking pan. Add about ½ inch of water to the pan and bake at 350 degrees for about 40 minutes, until the squash is just tender. Meanwhile, marinate the tofu in the soy sauce and sherry. Toast the bread cubes on a baking sheet for 5 minutes.

Sauté the onions and celery in 2 tablespoons oil, using a pot large enough for all the remaining ingredients. When the onions are translucent, add the mushrooms, marjoram, thyme, and stock or water. Cook covered for 10 minutes, then add the tofu with its marinade and the bread cubes. Sauté for another 5 minutes. Adjust the seasoning. Remove from the heat. Stir in the pecans and lemon juice.

Mound the filling in the baked squash halves and bake covered at 350 degrees for 20 minutes.

This cold weather dish is nicely accompanied by Scandinavian Apple Soup (recipe #3) and Squash Rolls (recipe #107). It is even more delicious topped with Light and Tangy Orange Sauce (recipe #91).

3 or 4 small winter squash (such as acorn or buttercup), halved and seeded
1 cake of tofu, pressed (*see Appendix*) and cut into small cubes
3 tablespoons tamari soy sauce
3 tablespoons dry sherry
4 cups small bread cubes

2 tablespoons vegetable oil
3 cups chopped onions
3 celery stalks, chopped
4 cups sliced mushrooms (1 pound)
½ teaspoon dried marjoram
¼ teaspoon dried thyme
½ cup Vegetable Stock (recipe #17) or water
1 cup pecans, toasted and chopped
1 tablespoon fresh lemon juice

CHILAQUILES

SERVES 4 TO 6

This is the perfect dish to prepare with leftover refried beans and spicy chili. In fact, this dish is such a fine tasting casserole that you may want to make it from scratch, which will be time-consuming at first, but worth consuming in the end!

✣ ✣ ✣

Sauté the onions in the oil until they are translucent. Add the peppers and continue to sauté until the peppers soften. Stir occasionally. To assemble the casserole, line the bottom of a well-oiled 12 x 12-inch casserole dish with broken tortillas or tortillas chips. Then spread on a thick layer of refried beans. Cover the bean layer with the sautéed onions and peppers. Sprinkle on the chopped olives, if desired. Ladle on the Salsa Cruda. Top with the grated cheddar.

Bake covered at 375 degrees for 30 to 35 minutes, until the cheese is bubbly. Then uncover the casserole and allow it to bake 5 to 10 minutes more until the edges begin to brown.

Serve with Arroz Verde (recipe #93) or Guacamole (recipe #40).

2 tablespoons vegetable oil
2 cups chopped onions
2 medium green peppers, chopped

8 corn tortillas, brushed with oil and baked until crisp, or 1 medium bag of tortilla chips
4 cups refried beans
2 cups Salsa Cruda (recipe #92)
⅓ cup chopped Spanish olives (*optional*)
1 cup grated sharp cheddar cheese (3 ounces)

MUSHROOM-LEEK FRITTATA

SERVES 6

Less exacting than a soufflé but lighter in texture than a casserole. This baked frittata is nice for brunch.

✤ ✤ ✤

Toast the bread cubes on a tray in a 375-degree oven. Meanwhile, lightly sauté the garlic in 2 tablespoons each of the butter and the olive oil until the garlic is golden. When the bread cubes are crispy, remove them from the oven, toss with the garlic butter, and set aside.

Next, sauté the leeks in the remaining 1 tablespoon each of butter and oil for a minute or two. Add the mushrooms, herbs, salt, and pepper and continue to cook, stirring occasionally. Cover the pan to retain the juices.

Preheat the oven to 375 degrees.

Butter a 9 x 9-inch pan. Layer ingredients as follows: first the bread cubes, next the cream cheese, then the vegetables, and finally the grated cheddar cheese. Beat together the eggs and milk with some salt and pepper and pour this over the other ingredients in the pan. Bake until the frittata is puffy and golden, about 30 minutes. Serve immediately.

You can also try this dish with broccoli and onions, asparagus and scallions–you name it. The cheddar may be replaced by a more exotic cheese such as Gruyère or fontina.

Serve with Tomato-Garlic Soup (recipe #5) and a crisp green salad.

1½ cups whole wheat bread cubes
3 tablespoons butter
3 tablespoons olive oil
2 medium garlic cloves, minced or pressed
1 cup chopped leeks (see Appendix)
3 cups sliced mushrooms (12 ounces)
1 tablespoon fresh dill or marjoram (1 teaspoon dried)
salt and black pepper to taste

4 ounces cream cheese, in ½-inch cubes
1¼ cups grated sharp cheddar cheese (4 ounces)
4 eggs
1¼ cups milk

POTATO KUGEL

SERVES 4 TO 6

David Hirsch's childhood featured holidays at Aunt Clara's in Borough Park, Brooklyn. One of the best parts of his visit was the promise of tasting again this crispy potato dish.

✳ ✳ ✳

Coarsely grate the potatoes using the largest side of a hand grater or the large-holed grater blade of a food processor. Remove the potatoes to a colander and squeeze out as much water as possible.

Preheat the oven to 350 degrees.

Grate the onions on the finer side of the grater or with the appropriate processor blade. Beat the eggs in a large bowl. Add the potatoes, onions, salt, pepper, and matzoh meal or bread crumbs. Mix well.

Put the oil in a 12 x 12-inch or 9 x 13-inch baking pan and place it in the hot oven for 5 minutes. Pour the hot oil into the batter, stirring just a little, and then pour the batter into the hot pan. This procedure makes the kugel crusty. Bake for 1 hour or until lightly browned.

Potato Kugel is a good side dish for large holiday meals or for supper at home. In either instance serve it (how else?) with sour cream and applesauce.

5 medium potatoes (2½ pounds), peeled if desired
2 medium onions
4 eggs
1 teaspoon salt
black pepper to taste
¼ cup matzoh meal (*see Appendix*) or bread crumbs
¼ cup vegetable oil

TORTINO DI VERDURE
(An Italian Vegetable Casserole)

SERVES 4 TO 6

L ayered vegetables and cheese baked together create a lavish and colorful production, like a lusty Italian opera.

✤ ✤ ✤

Slice the eggplant crosswise into ½-inch rounds. Place the eggplant rounds on a lightly oiled baking sheet. Bake covered with foil at 400 degrees until they are tender, about 45 minutes. Slice the potato and boil until just tender. Then drain and set aside. Slice the zucchini into ¼-inch rounds, slice the tomatoes about ½-inch thick, and set aside.

Mix together the bread crumbs, basil, and parsley. In a separate bowl, lightly beat the eggs with the salt and pepper.

Oil a 9 x 13-inch baking pan and coat the bottom and sides of the pan with about a quarter of the bread crumb mixture.

To layer the casserole, begin with all the eggplant slices. Drizzle 2 tablespoons of olive oil over them and sprinkle on a quarter of the bread crumbs and a quarter of the mozzarella and Parmesan cheeses. Pour a quarter of the beaten eggs on top of the cheese. Next layer all the potato slices. Repeat a layer of oil, crumbs, cheeses, and eggs. Layer all the zucchini, followed by oil, crumbs, cheeses, and eggs. Finally, layer the tomato slices topped with the remaining oil, crumbs, cheeses, and eggs.

Bake covered at 375 degrees for 45 minutes. Allow the casserole to sit for about 10 minutes before serving.

1 medium eggplant
1 large potato
1 medium zucchini
4 fresh tomatoes

1 cup bread crumbs
2 tablespoons chopped fresh basil (2 teaspoons dried)
3 tablespoons chopped fresh parsley

3 eggs
1 teaspoon salt
black pepper to taste

½ cup olive oil
1½ cups grated mozzarella cheese (6 ounces)
1 cup freshly grated Parmesan cheese (2½ ounces)

ZUCCHINI-FETA CASSEROLE

SERVES 4 TO 6

One of our favorites, a dish that exemplifies the good flavors of Balkan cuisine: tangy feta cheese, nutty bulgur, and herbed zucchini. We add a few tastes foreign to the Balkans, too: tamari and cheddar cheese.

✤ ✤ ✤

Place the bulgur in a bowl and pour the boiling water over it. Cover and set it aside until it has absorbed the water and become soft and chewable.

Sauté the onions and garlic in the oil until the onions are just translucent. Add the zucchini, dried herbs, and black pepper and continue to sauté on medium to low heat until the zucchini is tender, but not falling apart.

In a bowl, lightly beat the eggs. Mix in the feta and cottage cheese. Add the chopped parsley, tomato paste, and soy sauce to the bulgur and mix well.

Assemble the casserole in an oiled 9 x 9-inch casserole dish. Layer first the bulgur mixture, next the sautéed vegetables, and then the feta mixture. Top the casserole with grated cheddar cheese, tomato slices, and a light sprinkling of sesame seeds.

Bake covered at 350 degrees for 45 minutes. For crustier cheese, uncover the casserole for the final 15 minutes of baking. This casserole can be more easily served after it sits for 5 or 10 minutes. Serve with a tossed salad.

¾ cup bulgur (*see Appendix*)
¾ cup boiling water

2½ tablespoons vegetable oil
2 cups sliced onions
4 garlic cloves, minced or pressed
6 cups thinly sliced zucchini rounds
½ teaspoon dried oregano
½ teaspoon dried basil
½ teaspoon dried marjoram
⅛ teaspoon black pepper

2 eggs
1 cup grated feta cheese (5 ounces)
1 cup cottage cheese

½ to 1 cup chopped fresh parsley
2 tablespoons tomato paste
1 tablespoon tamari soy sauce

1 cup grated cheddar cheese (3 ounces)
2 medium tomatoes, thinly sliced
1½ tablespoons sesame seeds (*optional*)

SZECHUAN SAUTÉ

This is a basic Asian sauté with the additional zing of orange juice. The anise and Szechuan peppercorns add an authentic spicy flavor.

✳   ✳   ✳

Combine all the sauce ingredients except the cornstarch. Pour the sauce over the pressed and cubed tofu and allow it to marinate at least 15 minutes. Drain the marinated tofu, reserving the sauce. Stir the dissolved cornstarch into the sauce.

Heat the oil in a wok or large skillet. Add the grated ginger and stir for a minute. Add the snow peas and stir-fry them for just a minute. If you're using broccoli, stir-fry it until crisp, but tender, about 5 minutes. Stir in the marinated tofu. Slowly pour the sauce into the wok, stirring and simmering gently until it thickens, about 5 minutes. Stir in the peanuts. Sprinkle the sauté with a few drops of chili oil for a hotter dish. Serve immediately.

Serve on rice, garnished with chopped scallions.

2 cakes of tofu, pressed (*see Appendix*) and cubed

SAUCE
⅓ cup tamari soy sauce
½ cup dry sherry
½ cup orange juice
½ teaspoon ground anise or fennel seeds
½ teaspoon Szechuan peppercorns, roasted and ground (*see Appendix*)
1 tablespoon grated fresh ginger root
1 teaspoon dark sesame oil (*see Appendix*)

2 tablespoons cornstarch, dissolved in ½ cup cold water

¼ cup vegetable oil
1 tablespoon grated fresh ginger root
1 pound snow peas, stemmed, or 1 large bunch broccoli, cut into florets and stem pieces
1 cup toasted peanuts
hot chili oil (*optional*)

2 scallions, chopped

"BARBECUED" TEMPEH OR TOFU

SERVES 4 TO 6

Not the classic BBQ, but spicy and delicious in its own right.

✣   ✣   ✣

FOR TEMPEH:

Sauté the onions, garlic, and spices until the onions begin to soften. Add the peppers and tempeh and continue sautéing until the peppers brighten and the tempeh browns. Transfer this mixture to a shallow baking pan.

Whisk together the sauce ingredients and pour them over the vegetable-tempeh mixture. Bake covered at 350 degrees for ½ hour and uncovered for another ½ hour, stirring frequently throughout.

FOR TOFU:

Sauté the vegetables and spices. Whisk together the sauce ingredients. Combine the sautéed vegetables and the sauce and pour over the tofu cubes in a shallow baking pan. Bake as directed for tempeh, stirring very gently to avoid breaking the tofu cubes.

Serve on rice with a side dish of coleslaw or a green salad.

1 pound tempeh, cubed, or 3 cakes of tofu, pressed (*see Appendix*) and cubed

3 tablespoons vegetable oil
1 cup finely chopped onions
2 large garlic cloves, minced or pressed
1 teaspoon ground fennel seeds
1 teaspoon chili powder
1 teaspoon ground coriander
1 teaspoon ground cumin
⅛ teaspoon cayenne
1 green or red bell pepper, chopped

SAUCE
2 tablespoons tamari soy sauce
2 tablespoons fresh lemon juice
3 tablespoons molasses or brown sugar
2 tablespoons cider vinegar
1 tablespoon prepared mustard
6 tablespoons tomato paste (7-ounce can)
1 cup water
4 to 5 dashes hot sauce

"MAPO" TOFU

SERVES 4 TO 6

Inspired by the cuisine of Szechuan, this spicy dish is substantial and full of flavor. Our meatless variation of this classic has become a favorite at the restaurant among our "hot" food lovers.

✢   ✢   ✢

Press the tofu and then cut it into 1-inch cubes and set aside. Whisk together the sauce ingredients and set aside.

Heat the oil in a wok on medium to high heat. Sauté the onions for 3 to 4 minutes, stirring often. Then add the broccoli and sauté for an additional 4 minutes. Next add the mushrooms and cook for about 3 minutes, still stirring often. Pour in the sauce and add the tofu. Lower the heat, cover, and simmer until the tofu is thoroughly heated. Finally, add the dissolved cornstarch and bring back to a simmer, stirring occasionally until the sauce thickens.

Serve on rice, garnished with walnuts and scallions.

2 cakes of tofu, pressed (*see Appendix*) and cubed

SAUCE
¼ cup tamari soy sauce
¼ cup dry sherry
2 tablespoons white or cider vinegar
1½ tablespoons grated fresh ginger root
3 tablespoons tomato paste
1 cup water
1 tablespoon dark sesame oil (*see Appendix*)
1 to 2 tablespoons chili paste with garlic (*see Appendix*) or 3 garlic cloves, pressed, and cayenne to taste
¼ cup vegetable oil
2 cups thinly sliced onions
1 large bunch broccoli, cut into 3-inch spears
4 cups sliced mushrooms (1 pound)
2 tablespoons cornstarch dissolved in 2 tablespoons cold water

toasted walnuts
3 scallions, diagonally sliced

SWEET AND SOUR VEGETABLES AND TOFU

SERVES 4 TO 6

S weet and sour combinations are always a favorite at Moosewood and this particular one features tender-crisp vegetables with a zesty sauce.

✳   ✳   ✳

Stir together the sauce ingredients and set aside, and prepare the tofu and vegetables before you begin to stir-fry.

Heat the oil in a wok or a pot large enough for all the ingredients. Stir-fry the onions and ginger. When the onions are translucent, add the carrots and continue cooking for 3 to 4 minutes before adding the beans (2 more minutes), the pepper (2 more minutes), and then the mushrooms and zucchini.

Turn down the heat, cover the wok or pot, and cook, stirring once or twice, until the vegetables are tender but still crisp. Stir in the pineapple, tofu, sauce, and dissolved cornstarch and bring to a boil. Simmer, stirring gently, for 3 or 4 minutes. If a hot and spicy dish is desired, add a few dashes of hot chili oil.

Serve at once over rice or noodles. Top with sliced scallions.

2 cakes of tofu, pressed (see Appendix) and cubed

SAUCE
1½ teaspoons grated ginger
4 tablespoons brown sugar or honey
6 tablespoons white vinegar
3 tablespoons tamari soy sauce
¼ cup tomato paste or catsup

3 tablespoons vegetable oil
3 cups thinly sliced onions
1 tablespoon grated ginger
2 medium carrots, sliced long
½ pound string beans, whole, if small, or cut into 3-inch pieces
1 large red or green pepper, sliced long
4 cups sliced mushrooms
4 cups zucchini rounds
¾ cup chunks fresh or canned pineapple
1 tablespoon cornstarch dissolved in ½ cup cold Vegetable Stock (recipe #17), pineapple juice, or water
hot chili oil (optional)
2 scallions, chopped

VEGETABLE RAGOÛT

SERVES 4 TO 6

A crusty loaf of French bread is de rigueur along with a hearty burgundy, a wedge of Brie, and Edith Piaf. Or, for the peasant in you, serve over noodles with sour cream and Rachmaninoff.

✢   ✢   ✢

Heat the oil in a heavy stew pot or kettle (not aluminum or cast iron because tomato and wine react chemically with these metals). Sauté the garlic, onions, carrots, celery, and green beans for 3 to 4 minutes. Add the bay leaves, thyme, and red wine and boil, uncovered, for 3 minutes. Reduce heat, cover, and simmer for 5 minutes. Add the zucchini and mushrooms. Combine the sauce ingredients and then stir the sauce into the vegetables. Simmer approximately 30 minutes, until the vegetables are tender and the flavors well blended.

While the vegetables are stewing, cook the potatoes separately in salted, boiling water until they are tender. Drain and add them to the ragoût a few minutes before serving.

2 tablespoons vegetable oil
2 garlic cloves, minced or pressed
2 cups chopped onions
2 medium carrots, sliced in ½-inch pieces
4 medium celery stalks, chopped
1½ cups cut green beans
2 bay leaves
pinch of dried thyme
1½ cups dry red wine
1½ cups sliced zucchini
4 cups sliced mushrooms (1 pound)

SAUCE

2 tablespoons tamari soy sauce
½ teaspoon salt
1 cup Vegetable Stock (recipe #17) or water
3 tablespoons tomato paste
1 teaspoon Dijon mustard
1 tablespoon vinegar
1 tablespoon molasses
pinch of black pepper
1 teaspoon dried basil (optional)

2 medium potatoes, cut in chunks

MOROCCAN STEW

SERVES 4 TO 6

The exotic fragrance of this dish as it's cooking is almost reason enough to make it. This vegetable stew makes a substantial meal, especially when served with hard-boiled eggs, almonds, and couscous or pita bread, which is how we always serve it at the restaurant.

✣   ✣   ✣

In a stew pot, heat the olive oil and sauté the onions for 2 or 3 minutes. Add the garlic and spices, stirring continuously. Add the vegetables in the order given above, so that the starchier vegetables will cook the longest. Sauté after the addition of each vegetable until its color deepens. Stir in the garbanzo beans, the saffron, and the currants or raisins. There should be some liquid at the bottom of the pot from the cooking vegetables. However, if the stew is dry, add ½ cup of tomato juice, liquid from the garbanzo beans, or water.

Cover the stew and simmer on low heat until the vegetables are tender. Add the chopped parsley just before serving.

⅓ cup olive oil
3 cups coarsely chopped onions
2 garlic cloves, minced or pressed
1 teaspoon ground cumin
1 teaspoon turmeric
½ teaspoon cinnamon
¼ to 1 teaspoon cayenne
½ teaspoon paprika

1 cup sliced carrots
4 cups cubed sweet potatoes or butternut squash
3 cups cubed eggplant
1 green pepper, sliced in strips
4 cups sliced zucchini or summer squash
2 large tomatoes, chopped
1½ cups cooked garbanzo beans (*see Appendix*), liquid reserved
pinch of saffron
¾ cup dried currants or ½ cup raisins

¼ cup chopped fresh parsley

WEST AFRICAN GROUNDNUT STEW

SERVES 4 TO 6

The recipe for this stew came from Sierra Leone, Africa and then underwent a few changes in the Moosewood kitchen. To be authentic, the dish would use palm oil, tomato paste, and fewer vegetables, but with all due respect, we prefer our version.

✳ ✳ ✳

Steam or boil the sweet potato cubes until just tender.

Meanwhile, sauté the garlic, ginger, and spices in oil for one minute. Add the onions and cook until they begin to soften. Add the tomatoes, eggplant, and a small amount of vegetable stock or water and simmer for 10 minutes. Add the zucchini and peppers and continue to simmer until all of the vegetables are tender, about 20 minutes.

Drain the sweet potatoes and add them to the stew along with the tomato juice and peanut butter. Stir well. Simmer on very low heat for 5 to 10 minutes, stirring occasionally to prevent sticking.

Serve on rice, couscous, or millet. At Moosewood we garnish this stew with hard-boiled egg halves and pineapple and banana slices.

2 sweet potatoes, peeled and cubed

2 tablespoons vegetable oil
3 garlic cloves, minced or pressed
3 tablespoons grated fresh ginger root
2 tablespoons ground coriander
½ teaspoon cayenne (or to taste)
4 cups chopped onions
2 tomatoes, chopped
4 cups peeled and cubed eggplant
¼ to ½ cup Vegetable Stock (recipe #17) or water
1 cup chopped zucchini or yellow summer squash
2 green peppers, coarsely chopped

2 cups tomato juice
½ cup peanut butter

ZUCCHINI ANKARA

SERVES 4 TO 6

An unusual Mediterranean-style dish with a bright lemony flavor.

✜ ✜ ✜

Sauté the onions and garlic until the onion is translucent. Add the squash and marjoram and cook on medium heat, stirring often, until the squash is just tender. If the squash hasn't released enough liquid to simmer in, add ¼ cup of water. This should be a juicy dish. Add the garbanzos, olives, cumin or mint, lemon juice, and seasonings. Remember that if the feta that will be sprinkled on top later is quite salty, little or no salt will be needed in the vegetables themselves. Continue cooking until everything is thoroughly heated. The squash should not become overly soft.

Adjust the lemon and herbs to taste and ladle the vegetables over the rice or couscous. Top with feta cheese and serve immediately.

¼ cup olive oil
2 cups chopped onions
3 to 4 garlic cloves, minced or pressed
3 zucchini and/or yellow squash, cut into half-moons about ½-inch thick (about 6 cups total)
1 teaspoon dried marjoram
1 cup cooked drained garbanzo beans (see Appendix)
½ cup sliced, pitted black olives (preferably salty Greek ones)

1 tablespoon ground cumin or 2 teaspoons dried mint
3 to 6 tablespoons fresh lemon juice
salt and black pepper to taste
pinch of cayenne

1 cup grated feta cheese (5 ounces)

MIXED VEGETABLE CURRY

Serves 4 to 6

Cinnamon, cardamom, turmeric, cumin . . . the beginning of curry. Traditionally, curries are served with a variety of condiments and side dishes. See our suggestions at the end of the recipe.

✳ ✳ ✳

Melt the butter and oil in a skillet or wok. Add the mustard seeds and heat until they begin to pop. Add the remaining spices and cook on low heat for a couple of minutes to enhance the flavors of the spices. Be very careful not to burn them. Add the chopped onions and sauté until translucent.

Add the carrots and cook several minutes. Add the potatoes and cook a few minutes more. Add the cauliflower and stir well to coat all the vegetables with the spice mixture. Add the water, cover the pan, and simmer about 20 minutes, stirring occasionally. When the potatoes are tender but not completely cooked, add the tomatoes and peas or green peppers. Simmer covered for 10 to 15 minutes longer. The vegetables should retain their bright color, and if you use sweet potatoes, they will soften and become part of the sauce making it thicker and more interesting.

Serve on plain or Coconut Rice (recipe #94). Garnish with yogurt, cashews, raisins or currants, and banana slices. Accompany with Peach Chutney (recipe #103).

2 tablespoons vegetable oil
3 tablespoons butter
½ teaspoon black mustard seeds (*optional*)
3 medium garlic cloves, minced or pressed
1 teaspoon cinnamon
½ teaspoon ground cardamom
1½ teaspoons ground cumin
1½ teaspoons ground coriander seeds
1½ teaspoons ground fennel seeds
1 teaspoon turmeric
2 teaspoons grated fresh ginger root
½ teaspoon cayenne (or more to taste)
1 teaspoon salt
2 cups chopped onions (*optional*)
2 medium carrots, sliced into half-moons
3 cups cubed sweet potatoes or white potatoes

(more)

Moosewood is more than a restaurant; it is an enhancement of our civilization. And, of course, as a gardener, I rush home to try to apply the principles of both restaurant and book to my own produce.

–Peter Hedrick
baroque oboist and professor at Ithaca College

1 medium head of cauli-
   flower, cut into florets
¾ cup water
2 medium tomatoes,
   chopped
2 cups green peas or 2
   medium green peppers,
   chopped

2 cups plain yogurt
½ cup cashews, lightly
   toasted
½ cup raisins or currants
1 banana

CREOLE BEANS AND RICE

SERVES 6

Our version of a New Orleans classic. Traditionally prepared on Mondays, when the washing could be done while the beans simmered away on a back burner.

* * *

Cook the beans (*see Appendix*) with ½ teaspoon cayenne and ⅛ teaspoon ground allspice.

Combine all the salsa ingredients and set aside. After half an hour taste the salsa and add more hot pepper sauce if you'd like it "hotter."

Sauté the onions and garlic in oil on medium heat until the onions are translucent. Add the celery and carrots and continue to cook several minutes longer. Stir occasionally. Add the green pepper and sauté until all the vegetables are just tender. Whisk together the tomato paste, red wine, vinegar, brown sugar, mustard, herbs, and spices. Add this to the sautéed vegetables. In a large pot combine the drained beans and the sautéed vegetable mixture and stir them until thoroughly mixed. Simmer covered for 30 minutes, stirring frequently.

Cook the rice (*see Appendix*).

When both the beans and the rice are ready, prepare each plate individually with a layer of rice and then beans, topped with a spoonful or two of salsa. Finish with a dollop of sour cream, and get ready to warm your innards.

3 cups dried kidney beans
½ teaspoon cayenne
⅛ teaspoon ground allspice

SALSA
3 scallions, diced
1 cucumber, peeled, seeded, and diced
2 tomatoes, diced
¾ cup chopped fresh parsley
¼ cup vegetable oil
3½ tablespoons cider vinegar
salt to taste
Tabasco or other hot pepper sauce to taste

3 tablespoons vegetable oil
3 cups chopped onions
6 garlic cloves, minced or pressed
3 medium celery stalks, diced
1 cup diced carrots
2 to 3 green peppers, chopped
⅓ cup tomato paste

(more)

¼ cup red wine
1 teaspoon cider vinegar
1½ teaspoons brown sugar
1 teaspoon Dijon mustard
1¼ teaspoon salt
½ teaspoon dried oregano
⅛ teaspoon cayenne
⅛ teaspoon ground allspice

2½ cups uncooked brown rice
sour cream

CUBAN BLACK BEANS AND RICE

SERVES 6

Oh, Ricky, play Babaloo! Here's a well spiced, wholesome meal of contrasting tastes and textures. Rejoice over leftovers, because black beans taste great the second day and can be made into black bean soup simply by adding more tomatoes and orange juice.

✤ ✤ ✤

Drain the cooked beans and reserve the liquid.

In a large skillet or sturdy saucepan, sauté the onions, garlic, and spices in the oil or butter until the onions are translucent. Add the carrots and sauté for 3 or 4 minutes. Add the green peppers and sauté for 5 minutes more. Add salt, black pepper, parsley, juice, and tomatoes and simmer until the vegetables are tender.

Combine the drained black beans with the vegetable mixture. Purée 2 to 3 cups of the bean-vegetable mixture in the blender with enough reserved liquid (or stock or water) to make a smooth purée. Stir the purée into the beans and simmer for 10 minutes. Taste for salt.

Serve the beans on hot rice and top with a dollop of sour cream.

7 cups cooked black beans (see Appendix)

3 tablespoons olive oil or butter
2 garlic cloves, minced or pressed
1 cup chopped onions
1 teaspoon ground cumin
1 teaspoon ground coriander seeds
1 teaspoon paprika
1 cup chopped carrots

1 medium green pepper, chopped
salt and black pepper to taste
¼ cup chopped fresh parsley
1 cup tomato juice or orange juice
2 medium tomatoes, chopped
6 cups cooked brown rice (see Appendix)
1 cup sour cream

BOSTON BLACK-EYED PEAS

SERVES 4

Southerners have a special fondness for black-eyed peas. This treatment has a decidedly New England twist, but the distinctive flavor of the black-eyed peas still comes through. Black-eyed peas are traditionally served on New Year's Day to ensure good luck, and we ain't just whistlin' Dixie.

✤ ✤ ✤

Bring the salted water to a boil in a saucepan. Add the black-eyed peas. Cover and return to a boil, then lower the heat and simmer until just tender, about 15 minutes.

Sauté the garlic and onions in the butter or oil until the onions are just translucent. If you choose to add greens, mix them into the onions and continue to sauté until the greens wilt. Mix together the soy sauce, molasses, and mustard and set aside. Drain the black-eyed peas, saving a cup of the liquid.

In the saucepan, stir together the drained peas, the sautéed onion mixture and the molasses-soy sauce. Cover and simmer on very low heat for 10 to 15 minutes, stirring frequently. During this simmer there is some danger of sticking or scorching, so either use a "waffle" (*see Appendix*) or watch closely, adding a little of the pea stock if the sauce becomes too thick.

We like Boston Black-Eyed Peas served with tart coleslaw and Corn Bread (recipe #109) or Steamed Brown Bread (recipe #108).

4 cups fresh black-eyed peas (or 2 10-ounce packages frozen)
3 cups water
1 teaspoon salt

1 tablespoon butter or vegetable oil
2 garlic cloves, minced or pressed
1 cup chopped onions
1 cup chopped fresh beet greens, collards, chard, or spinach (*optional*)
¼ cup tamari soy sauce
⅓ cup molasses
1 teaspoon dried mustard or a good quality prepared mustard

PISSALADIÈRE

SERVES 4 TO 6

This Provençale quiche reflects the Mediterranean fondness for basil, tomatoes, and olives.

* * *

Roll out the pastry dough and line a 9-inch pie pan with it.

Sauté the onions and garlic in olive oil until tender and lightly golden. Add the basil and salt.

Preheat the oven to 375 degrees.

Thoroughly mix the eggs, milk, mustard, and flour and set aside. Combine the two cheeses. Sprinkle half of the cheese into the pie shell. Spread the sautéed onions over the cheese. Scatter on the sliced olives. Pour the egg-milk mixture into the pie. Cover with the remaining cheese and arrange the tomato slices attractively on top. Bake 40 to 45 minutes or until the custard is set.

Now, get out your red-checked tablecloth, open a bottle of wine, light the candles, imagine a soft Mediterranean breeze, and . . . .

pastry dough for one 9-inch pie (recipe #117)
2 tablespoons olive oil
2 cups chopped onions
1 garlic clove, minced or pressed
¼ teaspoon salt
3 tablespoons chopped fresh basil (1 tablespoon dried)
4 eggs, lightly beaten
1 cup milk
¼ teaspoon dry mustard
1 tablespoon unbleached white flour
⅓ cup freshly grated Parmesan cheese (1 ounce)
¾ cup grated mozzarella cheese, packed (4 ounces)
⅓ cup sliced, pitted black olives

1 medium tomato, thinly sliced

SOYFALAFEL

YIELDS APPROXIMATELY 36 SMALL BALLS

Falafel are the hot dogs of the Middle East. Stuffed into pita bread, Soyfalafel is street food, something to eat on the go. When made the traditional way with cooked garbanzo beans, preparation is a long process. Our version, using tofu, is much faster, equally delectable, and lighter and higher in protein.

✠   ✠   ✠

In a large bowl, mix together all the ingredients. Form into 1-inch balls and bake at 350 degrees on an oiled baking sheet for about 30 minutes. The balls should be golden and a little crusty on the outside, but still moist inside.

Serve with Tahini-Garlic Dressing (recipe #34). Soyfalafels make excellent appetizers and are also delicious stuffed into toasted pita bread with shredded lettuce, chopped tomatoes, cucumbers, and dressing.

- 3 cakes of tofu, pressed (*see Appendix*) and mashed
- 1 cup finely chopped onions
- 3 tablespoons vegetable oil
- 1 cup bread crumbs
- ¼ cup chopped fresh parsley
- 1½ tablespoons dark sesame oil (*see Appendix*)
- 3 tablespoons tamari soy sauce
- black pepper to taste
- 3 garlic cloves, minced
- ½ cup toasted sesame seeds
- 1 tablespoon ground cumin
- 1 tablespoon turmeric
- 4 tablespoons tahini (*see Appendix*)
- 4 tablespoons fresh lemon juice
- ¼ to ½ teaspoon cayenne

TOFU BURGERS AND "MEATBALLS"

YIELDS 6 LARGE BURGERS

Tofu burgers may sound like the early days of '60s vegetarian cooking, when imitation meat was all the rage. But in fact, these burgers are absolutely delicious and are one of our most popular standard lunch items. We know lots of kids who gladly devour tofu burgers and "meatballs."

✤　✤　✤

Sauté the vegetables and basil in oil until tender, about 10 minutes. In a large bowl, lightly beat the eggs, then add the bread crumbs, walnuts, and remaining ingredients. Mash the pressed tofu either with a potato masher or your hands and add it to the bowl, along with the sautéed vegetables. Stir well; the mixture should be firm enough to form into patties.

Pat the mixture into 6 large "burgers." Bake on an oiled baking sheet at 375 degrees until golden brown on the outside, but still moist inside, about 30 minutes.

Serve with your choice of dressing or ketchup, tomato slices, lettuce, pickles, chips, and sprouts on whole wheat or rye toast.

TOFU "MEATBALLS":

For about 3 dozen balls, add the following ingredients to the basic burger mix: 3 garlic cloves, minced, 1 teaspoon ground fennel seed, ¾ teaspoon dried oregano, and an addi-

3 tablespoons vegetable oil
1 large onion, finely chopped
1 large carrot, grated
1 green pepper, finely chopped
1½ teaspoons dried basil

2 large eggs* *(see note on back of card)*
1 cup bread crumbs
¾ cup walnuts, ground or finely chopped
¼ cup chopped fresh parsley
1 tablespoon Dijon mustard
1½ tablespoons dark sesame oil *(see Appendix)*
3 tablespoons tamari soy sauce
black pepper to taste

3 cakes of tofu, pressed *(see Appendix)*

tional 1½ teaspoons Dijon mustard. Form 1½-inch balls and bake at 350 degrees on an oiled baking sheet for 20 to 30 minutes.

When that urge for a submarine sandwich hits, stuff some pita or Italian bread with lettuce, bermuda onions, and Tofu "Meatballs" doused with tomato sauce. Or use them to top off spaghetti with tomato sauce and grated Parmesan cheese.

*For an eggless version, omit the eggs and add the juice of 1 lemon and ¼ cup tahini (see Appendix). Reduce the tamari soy sauce to 2 tablespoons and increase the bread crumbs to 1¼ cups.

KOLOKITHOPITA

(A Zucchini-Feta Cheese Strudel)

SERVES 6

Strudel is a snazzy centerpiece for any meal. This one has the added advantage of using up some of the mountains of zucchini that even the smallest garden seems to produce.

* * *

Place the grated zucchini in a colander, salt it lightly, and cover it with a plate that is weighted down with a heavy can. Allow the zucchini to drain for at least 20 minutes.

Sauté the onions and garlic in olive oil until the onions are translucent. Mix the cheeses, eggs, and flour in a large bowl.

Return to the zucchini. Take a handful at a time and squeeze out as much additional juice as possible. Add the zucchini, herbs, and spices to the pan with the onions and sauté gently for 10 minutes. Combine the sautéed vegetables and cheese mixture.

Preheat the oven to 350 degrees.

Assemble the strudel *(see Appendix)*. Bake for 45 minutes or until puffy and golden. Allow to rest 10 minutes before slicing.

Serve Kolokithopita with Tzatziki (recipe #98), Middle Eastern Carrot Salad (recipe #21), and glossy kalamata olives.

4 cups grated zucchini, (about 2 medium zucchini)

¼ cup olive oil
1½ cups chopped onions
2 garlic cloves, minced or pressed
2 cups grated feta cheese (10 ounces)
2 cups cottage cheese
4 eggs, lightly beaten
3 tablespoons unbleached white flour
1 tablespoon chopped fresh parsley
1 tablespoon fresh mint (1 teaspoon dried)
2 tablespoons fresh dill (1½ teaspoons dried)
½ teaspoon black pepper

½ pound phyllo dough *(see Appendix)*
¼ pound melted butter

RUSSIAN VEGETABLE STRUDEL

SERVES 8

Even if you have no Russian ancestors, these strong flavors seem to stir memories of a warm, steamy kitchen, safe from the bitter cold winds of the snowy steppes.

✳ ✳ ✳

In a large skillet or saucepan, sauté the onions in the butter and oil until they are translucent. Add the carrots and sauté for 5 minutes. Add the cabbage to the pan and sauté covered for another 5 minutes. Season with the salt, dill, and caraway seeds and cook for 5 minutes more. Add the mushrooms and black pepper and sauté for a final 5 minutes.

In a large mixing bowl, combine the softened cream cheese with the cottage cheese, grated cheddar, and eggs. Drain the sautéed vegetables and stir them into the cheese mixture.

Preheat the oven to 375 degrees.

Assemble the strudel (*see Appendix*). Bake for about 40 minutes, until golden brown. Allow the strudel to sit for 10 minutes before cutting.

Serve with cucumbers in Vinaigrette Salad Dressing (recipe #30) and a baked apple, and sigh for Mother Russia.

1 tablespoon butter
1 tablespoon vegetable oil
2 cups chopped onions
1½ cups thinly sliced carrots
3 cups chopped cabbage
1 teaspoon salt
1½ teaspoons dried dill
1 teaspoon caraway seeds
3 cups sliced mushrooms (12 ounces)
½ teaspoon black pepper

8 ounces cream cheese, at room temperature
2 cups cottage cheese
1 cup grated sharp cheddar cheese (3 ounces)
4 eggs

½ pound phyllo dough (*see Appendix*)
¼ pound melted butter

PASTAS

RECIPEASEL

ABOUT PASTAS

In some of the recipes which follow, we have specified a certain variety of pasta. Often we have not. Choose the pasta which you like best. As a general rule, long, thin pasta cuts (spaghetti, linguine, fettuccine) are best with a smooth, light sauce, and smaller cuts (shells or ziti) are more suited to a thick, chunky sauce. But you decide.

A pound of dried pasta generally serves 5 or 6, and a pound of fresh pasta serves 3 or 4. Cooking times vary according to the thickness of the pasta and whether it is fresh or dried and white or whole wheat. Fresh pasta cooks in just a minute or two, dried pasta usually takes 5 to 10 minutes, and whole wheat pasta may take up to 15 minutes. We prefer pasta cooked al dente, tender but firm.

To cook pasta, use a large pot and at least 1 gallon of water for each pound of dried or 2 pounds of fresh pasta. Bring the water to a rolling boil and add a tablespoon of oil to prevent the pasta from sticking together. Add a tablespoon of salt, and then add the pasta slowly, maintaining a steady boil. Stir frequently and test often for doneness. When cooked to your taste, drain the pasta immediately. If you're using it for a pasta salad, rinse with cold water. Otherwise, toss the drained pasta with a little butter or oil or some sauce and serve immediately. Warming the serving bowl and dinner plates is a gracious touch.

Experiment. Try new varieties and use old favorites in new ways. Add pasta to soups. Use it in casseroles. Fill your breakfast omelette with a leftover bit of spaghetti and sauce. Have fun with pasta–it's easy to cook, inexpensive, versatile, and delicious.

RAMATUELLE PASTA SAUCE

SERVES 4

This exuberant sauce is a seasonal favorite when honest tomatoes and fresh basil are available. The preparation is so speedy that you can put the water on to boil and then stroll out to pick the fattest, ripest tomatoes, still warm from the sun.

✤　✤　✤

Put the garlic, onions, basil, and tomatoes in a blender or food processor. Add the olive oil, salt, and pepper and blend until smooth. Set aside. This sauce is served at room temperature.

Heat the serving bowl and plates. Cook and drain the pasta. In the serving bowl, toss the hot pasta with some of the sauce. Serve the rest of the sauce and the grated Parmesan cheese at the table.

3 large garlic cloves, minced
⅓ cup coarsely chopped onions
1 cup fresh basil leaves, packed
5 or 6 large, ripe tomatoes, quartered
½ cup olive oil
salt to taste
¼ teaspoon black pepper

1 pound pasta

½ cup freshly grated Parmesan cheese

PASTA VERDE

SERVES 4

A bright green, protein-rich pasta sauce, a fine alternative to tomato sauce. Especially good with fettuccine, spaghetti, or egg noodles.

�֍ ✤ ✤

Sauté the onions and garlic in the oil until the onions are translucent. Rinse the washed, chopped spinach in a colander and then add it, still damp, to the onions. Cover the pan. When the spinach is wilted and still very bright green, purée the sautéed vegetables with the other sauce ingredients at medium speed in a blender or food processor. If you need to keep the sauce warm until the pasta is ready or if you reheat it later, use a double boiler to prevent curdling.

Cook and drain the pasta.

Toss the sauce with the hot, drained pasta in a warm bowl. Serve immediately, garnished with grated Parmesan cheese and chopped tomatoes or almonds, if desired.

2 tablespoons olive oil
¾ cup chopped onion
1 garlic clove, minced
3 cups coarsely chopped raw spinach
1 cup ricotta cheese (9 ounces)
1 teaspoon fresh lemon juice
1 tablespoon fresh basil (1 teaspoon dried)
½ cup chopped fresh parsley
¼ teaspoon nutmeg, preferably freshly grated
¼ teaspoon black pepper
½ teaspoon salt to taste

1 to 1½ pounds pasta

freshly grated Parmesan cheese
toasted and chopped almonds (optional)
chopped fresh tomatoes (optional)

FIVE EASY PASTAS

After a long day at work, when you feel tired and uninspired and the thought of stopping at the grocery store makes you groan, but there are probably a few edibles left in the refrigerator, fall back on the ease of a simple, improvised pasta dish. Here are five suggestions for tasty, nourishing meals that can revive your spirits in almost no time. Amounts and proportions are variable and are left to your judgment.

Just cook the pasta while you prepare the other ingredients. Toss the drained pasta with everything else, and it's ready!

#1
linguine or spaghetti
olive oil
garlic cloves, minced and sautéed in olive oil
freshly grated Parmesan cheese
chopped fresh parsley
black pepper

#2
any pasta
olive oil
Swiss chard, chopped and steamed or sautéed in olive oil
chopped fresh tomatoes
grated smoked Swiss cheese
black pepper

#3
any pasta
butter
red peppers, sautéed or steamed
sliced mushrooms, raw or lightly steamed or sautéed
green peas, lightly steamed
freshly grated Parmesan cheese

Use leftover pasta to make a "spaghetti pancake." Just toss the pasta with lightly beaten eggs, pour it into an oiled skillet, and gently fry until lightly browned. Flip it like a pancake and fry the other side. Salt and pepper to taste, sprinkle on some grated cheese, and you've got a quick little feast.

As a Moosewood customer for over 13 years, I have found Moosewood cooking to be always satisfying, often innovative, and at times, inspiring. Moosewood deserves credit for its fusion of a restaurant business with community politics and flat-out good food.

–Abby Nash
owner and chef, Abby's Restaurant and Catering

#4
spaghetti
butter
asparagus, cut into 1-inch pieces and
    steamed
heavy cream
freshly grated Parmesan cheese
black pepper

#5
soba noodles (*see Appendix*)
broccoli florets and sliced stems, steamed
sliced water chestnuts
thinly sliced carrots or celery, steamed or
    sautéed
cubes of tofu, blanched (*see Appendix*)
dark sesame oil (*see Appendix*)
tamari soy sauce
grated fresh ginger root
minced garlic cloves
chopped scallions

WINTER PESTO

SERVES 6 TO 8

Since fresh basil is not generally available year round, this pesto uses dried basil–a distinct advantage for satisfying cravings for pesto at any season.

✢ ✢ ✢

If you have time, soak the basil in the olive oil ½ hour before starting the recipe.

Wash and drain the spinach. Remove only the large stems. In a blender or food processor, blend half of the spinach with all of the lemon juice and half of the oil. Add the rest of the ingredients and blend until smooth.

Five years ago, when I moved my studio out of my house and into town, I included eating at Moosewood as part of the budget. I figure I've eaten there, say, 250 times since then, which must be close to a full day's output for the entire restaurant. That means I may have eaten a whole restaurant by myself. Frankly, I'm glad I did it in installments, but what I've noticed over the years is that they have lots of steady customers like me. And I have to say they're a healthy, good lookin' bunch of eaters.
–Tom Parker
from across the street, author of In One Day

4 cups firmly packed fresh spinach (about 5 ounces)
⅓ to ½ cup fresh lemon juice
½ cup olive oil
½ cup vegetable oil
⅓ cup pine nuts or chopped almonds or walnuts
¾ cup coarsely grated Parmesan cheese (2 ounces)
½ cup chopped fresh parsley
⅓ cup dried basil
2 garlic cloves, minced

SUMMER SAUCE FOR PASTA

SERVES 4

On those hot, lazy, sultry summer days, when, like a character in a Tennessee Williams play, you haven't got the energy to do much more than lie around the house in an old tattered slip, try this quick, uncooked sauce. It's fragrant, refreshing, and light.

* * *

Mix all the sauce ingredients together and let sit at room temperature for an hour or so, for the flavors to mingle.

Cook and drain the pasta. While the pasta is piping hot, serve it in well-warmed bowls, topped with a ladleful of sauce and garnished with Parmesan cheese.

6 ripe tomatoes
2 cups sliced mushrooms (8 ounces)
6 to 8 ounces mozzarella cheese, grated or cut into thin strips
½ cup chopped fresh basil
2 garlic cloves, minced
½ cup olive oil
1 teaspoon salt

1 pound spaghetti or linguine

½ cup freshly grated Parmesan cheese (1 ounce)

FISH

ABOUT FISH

Many of us never include fish in our diets. But those of us who do, recognize fish as a low-fat, high-protein food. At Moosewood we serve fish on the weekends, and it is an important part of our Sunday ethnic menus. On ethnic nights we explore the cuisines of different cultures and try ideas from our travels and varied backgrounds. So these recipes for fish reflect a global array of possibilities. You'll find them easy to prepare. A few will send you to a specialty shop where you can enjoy searching for the exotic.

We usually use flounder, scrod, sole, bluefish, cod, or haddock, all easily available fresh from Atlantic Coast markets. Allow ¼ to ⅓ pound of filleted fish per person. Fillets should be rinsed before cooking. When fish is to be baked, it should be placed in the baking pan skinned side down. The "skinned side" is the smoother, outer side of the fillet where the scales were. If baked with the skinned side up, the fillets sometimes curl, because the skinned side shrinks. When rolling fillets, the skinned side should be to the inside of the roll.

Baking time is a variable of the thickness of the fillets and the amount and density of the sauce or vegetables covering it. Fish is done when fillets have lost their translucency (and any hint of pinkness) and can be easily flaked with a fork. This is usually between 20 to 30 minutes when baked covered at 350 degrees.

CREOLE FISH STEW

SERVES 6 TO 8

This robust stew from Louisiana is animated by the Tabasco and lemon.

✢ ✢ ✢

Sauté the onions and garlic in the butter until the onions are translucent. Add the carrots, celery, and potatoes and sauté gently for 5 minutes. Add the zucchini and green pepper and sauté for 5 minutes. Add the bay leaf, thyme, tomatoes, tomato juice, and stock or water. Simmer 15 to 20 minutes, until the vegetables are tender.

Add hot pepper sauce, salt, and black pepper to taste. Stir in the lemon juice, fish, and shrimp. Simmer about 5 minutes until the fish is just cooked and flakes easily with a fork but does not fall apart.

Serve with chopped fresh parsley, lemon wedges, and hot pepper sauce. Wonderful with warm Corn Bread (recipe #109).

3 tablespoons butter or vegetable oil
1 cup chopped onions
1 garlic clove, minced or pressed
2 medium carrots, chopped
3 celery stalks, chopped
2 large potatoes, cubed
2 small zucchini, chopped
1 green pepper, chopped
1 bay leaf
pinch of thyme
1 cup chopped tomatoes
1 cup tomato juice
3 cups Vegetable Stock (recipe #17) or water
Tabasco or other hot pepper sauce to taste
salt and black pepper to taste
juice of 1 lemon
1½ pound firm, white fish, cut into bite-sized pieces
½ pound peeled and deveined shrimp

chopped fresh parsley
lemon wedges

JAPANESE FISH STEW

SERVES 8

This is a soothing, humble East Asian soup of fish with carrots, white cabbage, and shiitake mushrooms. Add green snow peas to the clear broth at the last minute and they will have cooked by the time you reach the table.

✢   ✢   ✢

Simmer the shiitake mushrooms in the water for 15 minutes. Drain, reserving the cooking liquid. Remove and discard the mushroom stems. Slice and save the mushroom caps.

In a large soup pot, sauté the onions in the oil until translucent. Add the carrots and sauté for a few minutes more. Add the Vegetable Stock and the reserved mushroom liquid and simmer until the vegetables are just tender. Add the fish cubes and the sliced shiitake mushrooms and simmer 5 to 7 minutes.

Combine the soy sauce, the wine or mirin, and the sesame oil and add to the stew when the fish is done. Add the snow peas and scallions and serve immediately.

For a hotter, spicier soup sauté some cayenne pepper with the vegetables and add some white vinegar and freshly grated ginger root.

8 dried shiitake mushrooms (*see Appendix*)
2 cups water

¼ cup vegetable oil
1 medium onion, thinly sliced
1 large carrot, julienned
2 celery stalks, diagonally sliced
¼ of a head of white cabbage, thinly sliced
½ teaspoon salt
8 cups Vegetable Stock (recipe #17)
1½ pounds bluefish or scrod fillets, cut in bite-sized cubes

4 tablespoons tamari soy sauce
2 tablespoons dry sherry, Chinese rice wine, or mirin (*see Appendix*)
1 tablespoon dark sesame oil (*see Appendix*)
½ pound snow peas, stems removed
3 scallions, diagonally sliced

TUNISIAN FISH SOUP

SERVES 6 TO 8

Moosewood's Nancy Harville Lazarus, inspired by dreams of North Africa and the fish soup served by our friends at Café des Amis in Ithaca, developed this recipe, a mix of vegetables, spices, and fish.

✤   ✤   ✤

Heat the oil in a large soup pot. Sauté the onions and garlic for 5 minutes. Add the carrots and sauté another 5 minutes. Add the peppers and the cabbage and stir the vegetables to coat them with oil. Sprinkle in the coriander and cumin and stir again. Cover and cook for 10 minutes.

Add the tomatoes, tomato juice, Vegetable Stock or water, lemon juice, and garbanzo beans. Cover and heat to a simmer. Simmer until the vegetables are tender.

Cut the fish into 1-inch chunks and add it to the simmering soup. Add hot pepper sauce and salt to taste. Simmer gently, just until the fish is white and flaky.

Serve with lemon wedges and toasted pita bread.

¼ cup vegetable oil
3 garlic cloves, minced or pressed
2 cups chopped onions
1 carrot, chopped
1 green pepper, chopped
4 cups finely sliced cabbage
1 tablespoon ground coriander
½ teaspoon ground cumin
3 cups finely chopped or crushed tomatoes, fresh or canned
1 cup tomato juice
2 cups Vegetable Stock (recipe #17) or water
⅓ cup fresh lemon juice
1 cup cooked drained garbanzo beans (see Appendix)

1½ pounds firm, white fish fillets
Tabasco or other hot pepper sauce to taste
salt to taste

1 lemon, cut into wedges

FISH À LA GRECQUE

SERVES 4 TO 6

This is a zesty, light, easily prepared dish. It's one of our favorite ways to bake fish because the flavors of the herbs, lemon, tomato, and feta harmonize remarkably well.

✤ ✤ ✤

Place the fish in an oiled casserole dish. Top the fillets with the onion rounds and sprinkle them with the dill, pepper, parsley, lemon juice, chopped tomato, and feta cheese.

Bake at 350 degrees about 30 minutes, until the fish flakes with a fork.

Serve under an imaginary grape arbor with real rice or Greek Potatoes (recipe #96), creamy Tzatziki (recipe #98), and a bottle of Retsina.

2 pounds fish fillets

1 medium red onion, thinly sliced in rounds
1 tablespoon fresh dill (1 teaspoon dried)
black pepper to taste
1 tablespoon chopped fresh parsley
¼ cup fresh lemon juice
1 tomato, chopped
½ cup grated feta cheese (2½ ounces)

FLOUNDER FLORENTINE

SERVES 4 TO 6

Spinach, dill and almonds are the grace notes to the flounder here, one of our most popular dishes.

✼ ✼ ✼

Sauté the onions in the butter or oil until translucent. Add the chopped spinach and the dill and cook covered until the spinach is wilted. Remove from the heat, add the almonds and lemon juice, and allow to cool.

Rinse the flounder. Place each fillet, skinned side up (see *About Fish*), flat on a board. Spoon a small amount of the spinach filling onto each fillet and then roll it up. Place the rolled fish in an oiled baking pan and bake covered at 375 degrees for 20 to 25 minutes, until the fish is tender and flaky.

Flounder Florentine is delicious served with Artichoke Heart and Tomato Salad (recipe #22).

2 tablespoons vegetable oil or butter
¼ cup finely chopped onions
10 ounces fresh spinach, stemmed and chopped
1 tablespoon fresh dill (1 teaspoon dried)
¼ to ½ cup toasted almonds, finely chopped
1 tablespoon fresh lemon juice

2 pounds flounder fillets

FISH WITH CANTONESE BLACK BEAN SAUCE

SERVES 4 TO 6

Traditionally this dish is prepared in a bamboo steamer over a wok. The distinctive, pronounced flavor of Chinese fermented black beans is delicious in our oven-baked version, also, and requires only a baking pan.

✣ ✣ ✣

Soak the fermented black beans in the water for several minutes and then drain.

In a small bowl, mix together all the ingredients, except the scallions, and mash well. Place the rinsed fish fillets in an oiled baking pan. Spread the paste over the fillets, sprinkle with the chopped scallions, and bake covered at 350 degrees for 20 to 30 minutes.

Serve on rice with Asian Asparagus Salad (recipe #28) and a wedge of melon.

1½ to 2 pounds fish fillets

1 tablespoon Chinese fermented black beans
½ cup water
1 garlic clove, pressed or minced
2 tablespoons tamari soy sauce
2 teaspoons dark sesame oil (*see Appendix*)
1 tablespoon grated fresh ginger root
2 teaspoons Chinese rice vinegar (*optional*)
2 scallions, diagonally sliced

FISH THEBAUDIENNE

SERVES 4 TO 6

A West African-style baked fish that was developed by Celeste Tischler for one of our Sunday Ethnic Nights. The unusual blend of sweet potato, cabbage, tomato, and lemon is surprisingly delicious.

✤ ✤ ✤

Brown the onions in 1 tablespoon of oil, then add the chopped pepper. Sauté until tender. Purée the sauté in a food processor or blender with the tomato juice and tomato paste to make a smooth, thick sauce.

Sauté the sweet potato in 1 tablespoon of oil for 5 minutes, then add the cabbage. Cover and cook on low heat. Cook until just tender, then mix in the pimiento, tomato sauce, salt, and pepper.

Place the fish in an oiled baking pan. Sprinkle with salt, black pepper, and lemon juice. Spoon the sweet potato-tomato sauce over the fish. Bake covered at 350 degrees for about 30 minutes.

Serve on rice or couscous with fresh corn on the cob.

2 tablespoons vegetable oil
1 cup chopped onions
1 green pepper, chopped
⅓ cup tomato juice
⅓ cup tomato paste

1 large sweet potato, peeled and sliced into rounds
1 cup shredded cabbage
¼ cup pimiento slices

2 pounds firm fish fillets (the flavor and texture of too delicate a fish would be lost under this sauce)
salt and black pepper to taste
juice of 1 lemon

PESCADO VERACRUZ

SERVES 4 TO 6

This lively and aromatic fish dish is from steamy Veracruz. Listen for the horns of a mariachi band when you open the oven.

✤ ✤ ✤

Arrange the fish in an oiled baking dish. Salt it lightly and sprinkle with a few teaspoons of the lemon juice. Chill.

Sauté the onions, garlic, chili powder, ground cloves, cumin, and coriander in the olive oil until the onions are translucent, taking care not to burn the spices. Add the tomatoes, honey, olives, and the remaining lemon juice and simmer for 15 to 20 minutes.

Pour the sauce over the fish, top it with chopped parsley, and bake at 350 degrees until it is tender, 20 to 30 minutes depending on the thickness of the fillets.

Serve with Arroz Verde (recipe #93) and a chilled salad of steamed cauliflower with red pepper strips.

2 pounds fish fillets
¼ cup fresh lemon juice

3 tablespoons olive oil
1 cup chopped onions
1 large garlic clove, minced or pressed
1 tablespoon chili powder
¼ teaspoon ground cloves
¼ teaspoon ground cumin
¼ teaspoon ground coriander
3 cups canned whole tomatoes, drained and roughly chopped
1 tablespoon honey
1 cup pitted black olives, chopped
salt and black pepper to taste

chopped fresh parsley

FISH WITH BOUILLABAISSE SAUCE

Serves 6 to 8

Classic bouillabaisse is a stew of fish and shellfish. This sauce incorporates the same complex blend of herbs, saffron, wine, and vegetables, but in a simpler and less expensive fashion.

✳ ✳ ✳

Heat the olive oil in a 2-quart saucepan. Sauté the leeks or onions for 5 minutes. Add the peppers and sauté another 5 minutes. Add the thyme, fennel, salt, garlic, and tomatoes and simmer covered for 10 minutes. Add the remaining ingredients, reserving 2 tablespoons of chopped parsley. Simmer uncovered for 15 minutes.

Place the fish in an oiled baking pan. Pour on the sauce and bake covered at 375 degrees for approximately 20 minutes, until the fish flakes easily with a fork.

Serve on rice or couscous. Garnish with lemon wedges and the remaining chopped parsley.

2 tablespoons olive oil
1½ cups chopped leeks (*see Appendix*) or onions
2 green peppers, chopped
¼ teaspoon dried thyme
2 teaspoons ground fennel seeds
1 teaspoon salt
3 garlic cloves, minced or pressed
3 large tomatoes, chopped
1 cup undrained canned tomatoes, chopped
1 tablespoon grated orange rind
1 cup dry red wine
1 cup Vegetable Stock (recipe #17)
1 tablespoon fresh tarragon (1 teaspoon dried)
2 tablespoons fresh basil (2 teaspoons dried)
juice of ½ lemon
pinch of cayenne
pinch of saffron
¼ cup chopped fresh parsley

3 pounds fish fillets
lemon wedges

SPICY CARIBBEAN FISH

SERVES 4 TO 6

Annato seeds give both a warm flavor and a golden hue to this exciting, highly seasoned dish.

✣   ✣   ✣

Place the fish fillets in a lightly oiled, flat baking pan. Pour the marinade over them, cover, and chill for ½ hour.

Sauté the annato seeds in the oil for a few minutes, stirring constantly and making sure they do not brown. Remove the annato seeds from the reddish-orange oil and then add the onions, scallions, garlic, and hot pepper. Sauté for a minute or two before adding the tomatoes, herbs, and seasonings. Simmer for 5 minutes.

Pour off the marinade and cover the fish with the sauce. Bake at 350 degrees until flaky. This will take about 20 minutes for small or thin fillets and 30 minutes for thicker, larger ones.

Spicy Caribbean Fish is good served on Coconut Rice (recipe #94) and garnished with lime wedges and parsley. Sweet potatoes or fried plantains are a nice side dish, and don't forget a tall, cool drink.

2 pound fish fillets

MARINADE
⅓ cup fresh lime juice
⅔ cup water
1 teaspoon salt

SAUCE
2 tablespoons vegetable oil
1 teaspoon whole annato (achiote) seeds (*see Appendix*)
⅓ cup chopped onions
⅔ cup chopped scallions
3 garlic cloves, minced or pressed
1 fresh hot pepper, minced (or ½ teaspoon cayenne)
3 tomatoes, chopped (or 2 cups canned, drained)
⅓ cup chopped fresh parsley
½ teaspoon dried thyme
salt and black pepper to taste

lime wedges
chopped fresh parsley

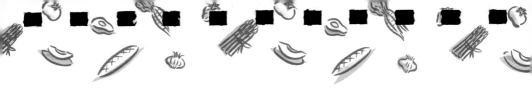

MALAY FRIED NOODLES WITH SHRIMP

SERVES 4 TO 6

A meal in itself. Accompany these fried noodles with sharp-tasting cold beer.

❋   ❋   ❋

First prepare the garnishes. In a wok or heavy skillet, heat the oil until it is very hot and stir-fry (*see Appendix*) the garlic for a few seconds until it is golden. Remove to a paper towel with a slotted spoon. Then stir-fry the onions in two batches until brown. Remove with a slotted spoon to paper towels. Slice the scallions diagonally in 1-inch pieces and set aside. Cut the fresh chili peppers into small circles, or if you're using dried chili peppers, simmer them in a small amount of water for 10 minutes and then chop.

Cook the noodles or pasta in boiling, salted water until just done. Drain and stir in the sesame oil to prevent the noodles from sticking together.

Reheat the oil in the wok. Add the garlic when the oil is very hot. A few seconds later add the shrimp. Stir-fry until the shrimp turn pink. Add the cabbage, snow peas, and water chestnuts and stir-fry for 2 minutes. Finally, add the cucumber slices and the cooked noodles and stir well. Remove from the heat and season to taste with soy sauce and black pepper.

Transfer to a warm platter and sprinkle with the garnishes or put each garnish in its own tiny bowl and pass with the noodles. Decorate with lime wedges if desired.

THE GARNISHES
- ¼ cup vegetable oil
- 2 large garlic cloves, thinly sliced
- 1 medium onion, thinly sliced lengthwise
- 2 scallions
- a few fresh or dried chili peppers

THE NOODLES
- 1 pound Chinese wheat noodles or vermicelli or spaghettini
- 1 tablespoon dark sesame oil (*see Appendix*)
- 2 garlic cloves, pressed or minced
- ½ pound shrimp, shelled and deveined
- ¼ of a small head of white cabbage, shredded
- 2 cups snow peas, stemmed
- ½ cup water chestnuts, sliced ¼-inch thick
- 1 medium cucumber, peeled, cut in half lengthwise, seeded, and sliced
- tamari soy sauce to taste
- black pepper to taste
- lime wedges

SAUCES, SIDE DISHES AND CONDIMENTS

SPICY PEANUT SAUCE

SERVES 4 TO 6

Can't get to Java this January? Here's a sauce that will warm you wherever you are in the western world.

✳   ✳   ✳

In a medium saucepan, brown the onions in oil with the bay leaf. Add the cayenne and coriander and sauté for a few minutes, stirring continuously. Add 2 cups of stock, coconut milk, or water and the lemon juice, vinegar, or tamarind. Simmer for 5 minutes. Add the peanut butter and salt, if needed, and simmer for another 15 minutes, stirring frequently to guard against sticking.

Check the seasonings. If you want a sweeter flavor, add the honey or brown sugar. If the sauce becomes too thick, add more liquid while it simmers.

This sauce has a multiplicity of uses. It is delicious over steamed broccoli, rice, and tofu. Leftovers can be cunningly incorporated into West African Groundnut Stew (recipe #63) or Mushroom-Sesame-Tofu Soup (recipe #9).

2 tablespoons vegetable oil, preferably peanut oil
2 cups chopped onions
1 bay leaf
1 teaspoon cayenne or to taste
1 teaspoon ground coriander seeds
2 to 3 cups Vegetable Stock (recipe #17), coconut milk (*see Appendix*), or water
2 tablespoons fresh lemon juice or white vinegar, or 1 tablespoon tamarind (*see Appendix*)

2 cups peanut butter
salt to taste
1 to 2 tablespoons honey or brown sugar (*optional*)

LIGHT AND TANGY ORANGE SAUCE

Y<small>IELDS</small> 2 <small>CUPS</small>

This golden sauce can be used 101 ways–it's also quick and easy.

✣   ✣   ✣

In a small saucepan, heat all the ingredients except the dissolved cornstarch. Bring to a boil and then whisk in the cornstarch. Cook for another minute. Serve hot.

Mushroom-Tofu-Pecan Stuffed Squash (recipe #51) is even more delicious topped with this orange sauce. Light and Tangy Orange Sauce is delightful on sautéed or steamed vegetables and simply baked fish. Try adding a little to Asian sautés and soups for an extra, interesting flavor.

2 cups orange juice
1 tablespoon freshly grated
   ginger root
1 tablespoon vegetable oil
pinch of thyme
1 teaspoon tamari soy
   sauce
4 teaspoons cornstarch,
   dissolved in 2 table-
   spoons cold water

SALSA CRUDA

YIELDS ABOUT 3 CUPS

An uncooked, speedily prepared tomato hot sauce with a clean, fresh taste and many uses. Depending on the amount and kind of peppers or chilies used, the intensity of hotness can range from mildly piquant to volcanic.

Combine all the ingredients and refrigerate at least 1 hour to allow the flavors to mingle.

Salsa Cruda is most flavorful at room temperature and should be taken from the refrigerator an hour before serving time. Use Salsa Cruda as a topping for frittatas or as a condiment for any Mexican entrée. Store in the refrigerator up to 1 week.

3 ripe tomatoes, chopped
¾ cup chopped Spanish olives
¼ to ½ cup minced hot peppers (fresh or canned)
Tabasco or other hot pepper sauce to taste

ARROZ VERDE

SERVES 6

Arroz Verde, green rice, complements a wide variety of foods. For a Latin flavor add 1 teaspoon ground cumin seeds. For a Mediterranean touch try 1 tablespoon capers (*see Appendix*) with 1 tablespoon either dill or basil.

✣   ✣   ✣

Purée the vegetables in a blender with ½ cup of water until smooth.

Sauté the rice in the oil for 2 or 3 minutes, stirring to prevent the rice from scorching. Add the vegetable purée and cook for 5 more minutes, stirring often. Add 3 cups of water and the salt and bring to a boil. Reduce the heat, cover, and cook until the liquid is absorbed, 30 to 45 minutes.

2 medium green peppers, chopped
½ cup chopped fresh parsley
1 medium onion, chopped
2 garlic cloves
½ cup water

2 cups uncooked brown rice
3 tablespoons vegetable oil
3 cups water
1 teaspoon salt

COCONUT RICE

SERVES 4 TO 6

This fragrant dish is rice dressed up in yellow with a hint of sweetness.

* * *

Sauté the rice, turmeric, and coconut in oil for 2 to 3 minutes. Stir constantly to coat everything with the oil. Add the water and the cinnamon stick. Cover the pot and increase the heat to bring the water to a rapid boil. It is best not to remove the lid while the rice is cooking, so when steam escapes from the pot, that is the signal to reduce the heat and simmer about 40 minutes.

Coconut Rice is especially handsome with curries and is a natural with Spicy Caribbean Fish (recipe #88) or Fish Thebaudienne (recipe #85).

- 2½ tablespoons vegetable oil
- 2 cups uncooked brown rice
- 1½ teaspoons turmeric
- ½ cup unsweetened coconut flakes
- 4 cups water
- ½ stick cinnamon

NORI ROLLS

Roseann Iacovazzi, our resident macrobiotic expert and teacher, showed us how to make nori rolls, those beautiful little seaweed rolls with a mosaic of vegetables in the center. And once you've gathered the more exotic ingredients and have mastered the rolling technique, Nori Rolls will become an easy, but ever so impressive, part of your repertoire, too.

Nori, wasabi, and bamboo rolling mats are all available at Asian food stores and many natural food stores.

✳ ✳ ✳

Cook the rice, using slightly more water than usual. The Japanese traditionally use a short-grained white rice, but we prefer brown rice. Leftover rice that has been reheated may also be used; cold rice will not roll properly.

While the rice is cooking, prepare the other ingredients. Some nori sheets are sold pre-toasted and should indicate this on the package. If yours aren't, toast them by passing each sheet lightly over an open flame. Mix about 1 teaspoon of the wasabi powder with water to form a smooth paste. Cover and set aside for a few minutes to allow the flavor to fully develop. Combine the vinegar, salt, and sugar and heat briefly to dissolve the sugar. Set aside to cool. Place the cooked rice in a large bowl, pour the vinegar mixture over it, and toss, using a wooden spoon or rice paddle, until the rice has cooled to approximately body temperature.

Place a nori sheet on the bamboo rolling mat. Moisten your hands and spread ¾ to 1 cup of rice evenly over the nori,

4 or 5 sheets of nori (see Appendix)
2 cups uncooked brown rice
4 tablespoons rice vinegar (see Appendix)
1 teaspoon salt
2 teaspoons sugar
vegetable strips for filling*
wasabi (see Appendix)
tamari soy sauce
special equipment: a bamboo rolling mat, called a *sudore*

*One or more of the following vegetables, all cut in thin strips: raw cucumber, avocado or scallions; lightly steamed green beans, carrots, red or green peppers; softened shiitake mushrooms (see Appendix). For an attractive filling, choose vegetables of contrasting colors, though you can use just one kind. Small amounts are adequate–1 carrot, cucumber, or pepper, 6 to 8 green beans, 3 or 4 scallions.

leaving a 1½-inch strip at the top edge uncovered. About 2 inches up from the bottom, make a horizontal groove across the rice and spread with a thin layer of wasabi. Place vegetable strips on top of the wasabi, in 3 lines, each line extending from edge to edge of the nori sheet. For example, if using avocados, carrots and scallions, make one horizontal line of each vegetable. If using only one vegetable, still lay down just three lines to avoid creating a fat, unwieldy roll.

Now, pick up the bottom edge of the mat and start rolling toward the top using firm and steady pressure to shape the roll. Some rice may be squeezed out at the sides. This can be corrected later, but do not allow the bare strip of nori at the top to be covered by rice or the roll won't seal properly. Most nori rolls are self-sealing, but if yours is being difficult, moisten the top edge of the nori sheet with a little water. Adjust the shape of the roll by squeezing gently on the mat. Set the nori roll aside. Repeat this procedure with the remaining sheets of nori, varying the fillings for interest.

With a sharp, wet knife trim off the ragged end pieces of the rolls, if necessary, and then cut each roll into 1-inch slices.

Arrange the slices cut side up on a platter and serve with small bowls of tamari soy sauce and additional wasabi for dipping.

GREEK POTATOES

SERVES 6

We cajoled the owner of the best Greek restaurant in town into giving us the basics of this recipe. Potatoes are baked with a lemon and garlic flavored marinade. The aroma alone is enough to set you dancing!

✢   ✢   ✢

Toss together the potatoes, lemon juice, oils, spices, and garlic in a deep, flat pan about 8 x 12 inches. Add the water. Bake uncovered for about 1½ hours at 475 degrees. Stir every 20 minutes adding more water if necessary to prevent sticking. Be very careful not to burn the potatoes during the last 30 minutes. During the final 15 to 20 minutes, allow the water to evaporate until only the oil is left.

Garnish with fresh parsley and serve.

Greek Potatoes are delicious alone or can be sprinkled with feta cheese and served with Egg-Lemon Soup with Spinach (recipe #11), roasted red bell peppers, and a green salad.

6 medium potatoes, cubed (3 pounds)
½ cup fresh lemon juice, about 2½ lemons
⅓ cup vegetable oil
1 tablespoon olive oil
2 teaspoons salt
½ teaspoon black pepper
1½ teaspoons dried oregano
2 garlic cloves, minced or pressed
3 cups hot water
chopped fresh parsley

ARMENIAN GREEN BEANS

SERVES 4 TO 6

A simple time-honored family recipe for preparing fresh green beans. Lemon and an assortment of herbs provide a brisk accent.

✳   ✳   ✳

Sauté the onions in the oil or butter until translucent. Add the beans and cook about 5 minutes, stirring frequently, until they turn a bright, shiny green. Stir in the tomatoes, lemon juice, herbs, and spices. Lower the heat and simmer, covered, 10 to 15 minutes, until the beans are tender and the flavors have married. Stir occasionally to prevent sticking.

2 tablespoons vegetable oil
2 cups chopped onions
3 cups green beans, whole or cut in half
4 medium fresh tomatoes, chopped or 1½ cups undrained canned tomatoes, crushed
3 tablespoons fresh lemon juice
⅛ teaspoon dried thyme
¼ teaspoon dried marjoram
¼ teaspoon dried basil
salt and black pepper to taste

TZATZIKI

SERVES 4 TO 6

Yogurt, cucumber, and mint all cool and refresh the palate.

Lightly salt the grated cucumbers, place in a colander or strainer, and set aside to drain for about half an hour.

In a bowl, combine the drained cucumbers with the rest of the ingredients. Chill for 30 minutes before serving.

Serve with Baba Ganouj (recipe #37). Hummus with Tahini (recipe #38), and pita bread. Tzatziki is a refreshing side dish with Fish à la Grecque (recipe #82).

2 large cucumbers, peeled and grated
2 garlic cloves, pressed or minced
2 cups plain yogurt
1 tablespoon fresh mint (¾ teaspoon dried)
salt and black pepper to taste

SWEET AND SOUR RED CABBAGE

SERVES 4 TO 6

An attractive and inexpensive side dish. You really don't need much sweetener, because well-cooked cabbage has a wonderful sweetness all its own.

❉   ❉   ❉

Sauté the onions in the oil or butter until lightly browned. Add the cabbage and continue to sauté for 5 to 10 minutes. Then add the rest of the ingredients except the honey. Cook on low heat, covered, for about 30 minutes, stirring occasionally. The cabbage will be greatly reduced in volume. Cabbage and onions are sweeter the longer they simmer, so taste first and then add more vinegar and the honey if needed.

We often serve this at the restaurant with its ethnic relatives Piroshki (recipe #43) or Russian Vegetable Strudel (recipe #73). If you serve it with a strudel already filled with flavorful herbs, you might choose to omit the dill and fennel and enjoy a simpler tasting sweet and sour cabbage.

2 tablespoons butter or vegetable oil
¾ cup chopped onions
6 cups thinly sliced red cabbage
¾ cup apple juice or cider
½ teaspoon salt
black pepper to taste
1 tablespoon fresh dill (1 teaspoon dried)
1 teaspoon whole fennel seeds
¼ cup raisins (*optional*)
3 tablespoons cider vinegar (more to taste)
1 tablespoon honey (*optional*)

MARINATED TOFU

SERVES 4 TO 6

Tofu flavored with a versatile marinade that's a bit more Chinese than Japanese, but useful in any East Asian cuisine.

❈   ❈   ❈

Place the tofu cubes in a strainer. Either pour boiling water over the tofu or dip the strainer into a pot of simmering water for 1 or 2 minutes. Set aside to drain thoroughly.

Whisk together all the marinade ingredients and add any of the optional ingredients that appeal to you. Pour the marinade over the tofu cubes in a large bowl and toss gently with a spatula. Chill at least 20 minutes before serving. A longer marinating time is fine, but we recommend that the tofu be served within a day for the texture to be at its best.

Serve Marinated Tofu as a side dish with any Asian meal or mix it at the last minute into stir-fried vegetables. Marinated Tofu is good as a topping for tossed or grain salads or as an addition to Miso Broth (recipe #4). Try frying it with leftover rice or noodles. Or stuff it into a pita and top with Spicy Peanut Sauce (recipe #90).

Use this marinade also with foods other than tofu. Vegetables marinated in this sauce are good skewered and roasted on a grill. Do the same with firm, oily fish, such as monkfish or bluefish. Or bake fish fillets marinated in this sauce.

2 cakes of tofu, pressed (see Appendix) and cut into ½-inch cubes

MARINADE
1 tablespoon fresh grated ginger root
2 tablespoons dry sherry, sake, or Chinese rice wine (see Appendix)
¼ cup tamari soy sauce
¼ cup water
1 tablespoon dark sesame oil
1 tablespoon rice, white, or cider vinegar

OPTIONAL INGREDIENTS
2 tablespoons minced scallions
½ teaspoon sugar or honey
½ teaspoon Szechuan hot bean paste or Chinese hot chili oil (see Appendix)
pinch of cayenne
1 teaspoon toasted sesame seeds

RECIPEASEL #100

KOREAN GREENS

SERVES 6

K orean Spinach is what Popeye eats when he is visiting Seoul.

✢ ✢ ✢

Prepare the sauce by mixing together the sesame oil, vinegar, soy sauce, and sugar.

Heat the vegetable oil in a wok or a large skillet. Add the greens and stir-fry until just tender, but not overcooked. Pour off any excess oil or liquid. Toss the greens with the sauce in a serving bowl. Sprinkle the sesame seeds over the greens and serve.

We like this dish best stir-fried, but if you wish to reduce your oil consumption, it may be prepared by cooking the spinach in ½ cup water until limp, draining it, and then proceeding as above.

Try this as a side dish with an Asian-style fish and rice.

2 pounds fresh spinach, stemmed and coarsely chopped (other greens may be substituted)
3 tablespoons vegetable oil

2 tablespoons dark sesame oil (see Appendix)
3 tablespoons white vinegar
3 tablespoons tamari soy sauce
a pinch of sugar (optional)
1 tablespoon sesame seeds, toasted

ITALIAN GREENS

SERVES 4 TO 6

The Italians traditionally prepare chard this way, and once you have experienced the simplicity and full flavor of this dish, so will you.

✤ ✤ ✤

Heat the olive oil in a wok or heavy skillet and sauté the garlic until golden. Remove the garlic with a slotted spoon and reserve. Add the greens and sauté until tender. Add the salt. Just before serving, sprinkle the reserved garlic over the chard.

Serve with Mushroom-Leek Frittata (recipe #53), pasta, or any mild-flavored entrée.

¼ cup olive oil
6 large garlic cloves, minced or pressed
12 to 14 large chard leaves and stalks, coarsely chopped (other greens may be substituted)
salt to taste

PEACH CHUTNEY

SERVES 6 TO 8

M̲ade with fresh, ripe peaches, this is a sweet-tart, spice-scented accessory to a curry dinner.

✳   ✳   ✳

In a saucepan, sauté the onions and garlic in the oil until the onions are golden. Add the peaches and vinegar and continue to cook covered, stirring frequently, until the peaches begin to soften. Add the honey and spices and simmer the chutney gently on low heat for 20 to 30 minutes more, until a chunky sauce consistency is reached.

Serve hot, or cool the chutney to room temperature before serving. Refrigerated, chutney will keep for at least two weeks.

2 tablespoons vegetable oil
1 cup finely chopped onions
2 garlic cloves, minced or pressed (*optional*)
10 ripe peaches, peeled, pitted and sliced
2 to 4 tablespoons cider vinegar, depending on sweetness of peaches
¼ cup honey
¼ teaspoon cinnamon
⅛ teaspoon nutmeg, preferably freshly grated
⅛ teaspoon ground cardamom
⅛ teaspoon cayenne
1 teaspoon grated fresh ginger root

BREADS

CRACKED WHEAT BREAD

YIELDS 2 LOAVES

A crunchy-textured change-of-pace with a warm grainy flavor.

✤ ✤ ✤

Read about bread making (*see Appendix*).

Generously butter two 5 x 9-inch loaf pans.

In a saucepan, cook the cracked wheat or bulgur in the water about 10 minutes until water is absorbed and the wheat has a gummy cereal consistency. Stir as needed to prevent sticking. Add the butter, salt, and molasses or honey.

Proof the yeast in the warm water.

Place the wheat mixture in a large mixing bowl and add the milk. When this mixture is lukewarm, add the yeast and stir. Add the whole wheat flour and beat well. Stir in white flour until the dough is stiff enough to knead.

On a floured board, knead the dough for 10 to 15 minutes, adding flour as necessary to prevent the dough from sticking. This will remain a very soft dough and should feel slightly tacky. Place the dough in a buttered bowl, turning to coat with butter. Cover and let rise until doubled, about 1½ hours. Cover your hands with flour and punch down. Knead the dough for 1 minute in the bowl and shape into 2 loaves. Place the loaves in the buttered loaf pans. Cover and let rise until doubled, about 30 minutes.

Bake in a preheated oven at 375 degrees for 30 to 35 minutes.

½ cup cracked wheat or bulgur
1½ cups water
¼ cup butter
4 teaspoons salt
¼ cup molasses or honey

1 tablespoon (or 1 package) dry yeast
⅓ cup warm water

1 cup milk
2 cups whole wheat bread flour
3½ to 4 cups unbleached white flour

SPICY CORNELL BREAD

YIELDS 2 LOAVES

Cornell breads were developed at the Martha Van Rensselaer School of Home Economics at Cornell University in the '40s during the beginnings of modern nutritional science. It was claimed that man could indeed live by (Cornell) bread alone. Any bread becomes a nutritious Cornell bread with the addition of powdered milk, wheat germ, and soy flour.

✤ ✤ ✤

Read about bread making (see Appendix).

Generously butter two 5 x 9-inch loaf pans.

Proof the yeast in the warm water.

Pour the hot milk over the salt, sugar, honey, and butter. Cool. Add the orange juice concentrate. Add the yeast and the eggs to the milk mixture. Stir in the spices, dry milk, soy flour, and wheat germ. Add the whole wheat flour and blend well. Stir in the white flour, turn out onto a floured surface, and knead 10 to 15 minutes.

Place the dough in a buttered bowl, turning it to coat it with butter on all sides. Cover and leave in a warm spot for 45 minutes to 1 hour, or until it doubles in bulk. Punch down the dough and knead it again for a minute. Cover and let it rise for 30 minutes. Punch the dough down, shape into two loaves, and place them in buttered bread pans. Cover the pans with a towel and let the dough rise until doubled, about 30 minutes.

Bake in a preheated oven at 425 degrees for 10 minutes and then at 350 degrees for 25 to 30 minutes more. Brush the tops of the loaves with melted butter or oil.

2 tablespoons (or 2 packages) dry yeast
⅓ cup warm water

2 cups milk, scalded (see Appendix)
1 teaspoon salt
¼ cup brown sugar
¼ cup honey
⅓ cup butter
⅓ cup orange juice concentrate
3 eggs, beaten
1 tablespoon ground cumin
dash of ground cardamom and/or ground coriander seeds
½ cup dry milk
1 cup soy flour
1 cup wheat germ
3 cups whole wheat flour
3 to 4 cups unbleached white flour

POTATO-ONION-RYE BREAD

Yields 2 loaves

This bread smells so good while it's baking that people will line up in the kitchen for the first slices.

✤ ✤ ✤

Read about bread making (see Appendix).

Oil two 5 x 9-inch loaf pans.

Proof the yeast in the warm water.

In a large mixing bowl, combine the onions, molasses, salt, oil, and caraway seeds. Pour the boiling water over the mixture and let it cool to between 105 and 115 degrees. Add the yeast, potato flour, and 2 cups of the white flour. Beat 300 strokes. Add the rye flour and enough of the remaining white flour to make a stiff dough.

Knead the dough on a floured surface for 10 to 15 minutes. The rye flour will make the dough sticky, so use more white flour if necessary to keep the dough from sticking to your hands. Place the dough in an oiled bowl, turn it to coat all sides well, cover with a cloth, and let it rise in a warm place until doubled in size, about 1 hour. Punch down the dough and let it rise for another hour. Punch it down again and shape into two loaves. Place them in oiled bread pans for the final 30-minute rising.

Bake in a preheated oven at 375 degrees for 40 to 45 minutes.

This bread is a perfect companion for Hungarian Vegetable Soup (recipe #6).

2 tablespoons (or 2 packages) dry yeast
½ cup warm water

2 cups finely chopped onions
3 tablespoons molasses
1 tablespoon salt
3 tablespoons vegetable oil
1 tablespoon caraway seeds
2 cups boiling water
1 cup potato flour (see Appendix)
4 to 5 cups unbleached white flour
4 cups rye flour

SQUASH ROLLS

Y<small>IELDS ABOUT</small> **15** <small>ROLLS</small>

S<small>pecial</small> fall and winter dinners deserve these treats. We call them "squash" rolls, but pumpkin or carrot will provide the same color and gentle sweetness. If you use fresh vegetables, boil or bake and then purée them. If you use frozen squash, thaw the squash and squeeze out any excess moisture. Canned carrots should be mashed, but canned pumpkin needs no preparation.

✤ ✤ ✤

Read about bread making *(see Appendix)*.
Generously butter a large baking sheet.
Proof the yeast in the warm water.
Combine the scalded milk, squash, sugar, salt, and melted butter. When this mixture has cooled to lukewarm, add the yeast and whole wheat flour. Beat well. Gradually stir in the unbleached white flour until the dough is stiff enough to knead. Turn onto a lightly floured surface and knead well, adding flour as necessary to prevent sticking. This is a soft, elastic dough and very pleasant to work with.

Place the dough in a large buttered bowl, and turn the dough to coat it with butter. Cover and let rise until doubled, about 1 hour. Punch down. Shape into tangerine-sized rolls and place them on the buttered baking sheet. Cover with a towel and let rise until doubled, about 30 to 45 minutes. Bake in a preheated oven at 400 degrees for 20 minutes. Brush the tops of the squash rolls with melted butter after removing them from the oven.

1 tablespoon (or 1 package) dry yeast
¼ cup warm water

⅔ cup milk, scalded (*see Appendix*)
1 cup cooked and puréed winter squash, pumpkin, or carrot
⅓ cup brown sugar
½ teaspoon salt
⅓ cup melted butter
2 cups whole wheat flour
2 to 3 cups unbleached white flour

STEAMED BROWN BREAD

YIELDS 2 LOAVES

Traditionally served with New England suppers, steamed brown bread is also terrific toasted and buttered for breakfast or with cream cheese as a sandwich for lunch.

✳ ✳ ✳

Generously butter two 1-pound coffee cans.

Sift the dry ingredients into a large bowl. Stir in the raisins. In a smaller bowl blend the buttermilk and molasses and pour into the dry ingredients, stirring just enough to moisten.

Fill each coffee can about two-thirds full. Cover tightly with aluminum foil. Place the cans on a rack in a deep kettle and pour in enough boiling water to come halfway up the sides of the cans. Cover the kettle and boil gently for 3 hours, adding more water as necessary.

Remove the cans from the water and remove the foil. If the loaves do not slide easily from the cans, place the cans in a hot oven (450 degrees) for 5 minutes. The hot oven treatment should cause the bread to shrink away from the sides of the cans and then slip right out. Keep Steamed Brown Bread refrigerated either in its cans or tightly wrapped in foil.

Serve Steamed Brown Bread for supper with Boston Black-Eyed Peas (recipe #68) and applesauce.

1 cup yellow cornmeal
1 cup rye flour
1 cup whole wheat flour
1 teaspoon salt
1 teaspoon baking soda
1 teaspoon baking powder
1 cup raisins

2 cups buttermilk
¾ cup molasses

CORN BREAD

YIELDS 12 PIECES

F ast and delicious.

❊   ❊   ❊

Preheat the oven to 350 degrees.

Generously butter a 9 x 13-inch baking pan or a 12-inch cast iron skillet.

Sift the dry ingredients into a large bowl. In another bowl, combine the wet ingredients and stir until mixed. Fold the wet ingredients into the dry ingredients. Smooth the batter into the baking pan or skillet and bake for 25 to 30 minutes, or until a knife inserted into the center comes out clean. Allow the corn bread to cool for at least 10 minutes before serving.

1½ cups yellow cornmeal
1 cup whole wheat pastry flour
1 cup unbleached white flour
1 tablespoon baking powder
1 teaspoon baking soda
1 teaspoon salt

2 cups buttermilk or plain yogurt
½ cup milk
¼ cup maple syrup or brown sugar
2 eggs, beaten
¼ cup melted butter, cooled

MUFFINS

It's early morning. You stumble into the kitchen. Your significant other has left a basket of warm muffins on the table. Love triumphs.

✣   ✣   ✣

Preheat the oven to 400 degrees.

Generously butter a 12-cup muffin tin.

In a medium bowl thoroughly mix the dry ingredients. In a smaller bowl lightly beat the egg with the milk, oil, and honey or sugar and add to the dry ingredients all at once, stirring until the batter is just barely mixed. Spoon the batter into the muffin tin. Bake for 20 to 25 minutes or until a toothpick inserted in the center of a muffin comes out clean.

VARIATIONS:

· *Blueberry Muffins:* Fold 1 cup drained blueberries (fresh, frozen, or canned) into the batter.

· *Cheese Muffins:* Add ¾ cup grated sharp cheddar cheese and omit the honey or sugar.

1¾ cups whole wheat pastry flour
2½ teaspoons baking powder
¾ teaspoon salt

1 egg
¾ cup milk
⅓ cup vegetable oil
¼ cup honey or sugar

ZUCCHINI-NUT BREAD

YIELDS 2 LOAVES

This sweet bread is moist and nutty when oven-fresh. Later try it toasted and spread with cream cheese.

✲ ✲ ✲

Preheat the oven to 325 degrees.

Oil two 5 x 9-inch loaf pans.

In a large mixing bowl, combine the oil and brown sugar. Add the eggs, one at a time, beating after each addition. Stir in the vanilla and zucchini.

In a smaller bowl, sift together the flours, cinnamon, salt, baking powder, and soda. Stir the dry ingredients into the oil and egg mixture until just moistened. Fold in the raisins and walnuts.

Spoon the batter into the prepared loaf pans.

Bake for about 1 hour, until a knife inserted into the center comes out clean.

1 cup vegetable oil
1 cup brown sugar
3 eggs
1 tablespoon pure vanilla extract
2 cups grated zucchini

1½ cups whole wheat pastry flour
1½ cups unbleached white flour
1 teaspoon cinnamon
1 teaspoon salt
1 teaspoon baking powder
½ teaspoon baking soda

1 cup coarsely chopped walnuts
1 cup raisins

DESSERTS

RECIPEASEL

WINE-POACHED PEARS

SERVES 6

This elegant, light dessert has origins in classic French and Italian cuisines. It's perfect after a rich pasta meal. The pears should be large and beautifully shaped. Virtually any variety will do, and the pears don't need to be perfectly ripe–in fact, they'll disintegrate a bit as they cook if they're not a little firm.

✳ ✳ ✳

Put the pears into a stainless steel pot large enough for an uncrowded single layer. Add enough poaching liquid to cover the pears so that they float and bob around. Add the sliced orange and the spices. Putting the spices into a tea ball or a piece of cheesecloth helps with clean-up later. Simmer on medium heat. Roll the pears over once or twice so that they poach evenly. Poaching time will vary depending on the variety, size, and ripeness, but will probably not take more than half an hour.

When the pears are tender and rosy-tinted, carefully remove them from the pot. Arrange them upright in a bowl. Add poaching liquid to about 1 inch deep and refrigerate. The remaining poaching liquid may be refrigerated for several weeks for a head start on the next batch. Or to be extra thrifty and efficient, use the leftover liquid to cook a selection of dried fruits for a succulent fruit compote.

Whip the cream with a little pure vanilla extract and sweetening until it's stiff.

Serve each pear on top of a generous scoop of whipped cream and spoon on a little of the poaching liquid.

6 whole pears, peeled, with stems intact
5 to 6 cups poaching liquid: red wine and fruit juice (pear, apple, apricot, or other) in any proportion
1 orange, sliced
1 cinnamon stick
a few whole cloves
several whole allspice

heavy cream, whipped with a little vanilla and maple syrup

APRICOT BAKLAVA

Y<small>IELDS</small> 24 <small>PIECES</small>

S̲weet and buttery, this traditional pastry of the Middle East is always made with honey and nuts. In our version, the unorthodox apricot custard layer in the middle comes as a welcome surprise.

✣   ✣   ✣

Simmer the dried apricots in the juice or water for about 1 hour. Remove from the heat and allow to cool. Purée the cooled, cooked apricots with the eggs in a food processor or in two batches in a blender.

Using a pastry brush or a small paint brush, butter a baking sheet. Unroll the phyllo dough. Carefully place two leaves of phyllo on the baking sheet. They should be flat and unwrinkled. Brush the top with butter and sprinkle with chopped almonds. Work quickly or keep the remaining unbuttered phyllo dough covered or it will dry and crack and become difficult to use. Continue this procedure until about half of the phyllo is used. Then spread the apricot purée evenly on the top layer of phyllo. Continue layering phyllo, butter, and almonds, ending with a buttered leaf of phyllo sprinkled with chopped almonds.

Before baking the baklava, score it with a sharp knife, cutting through the top few layers, but not as deep as the custard layer, to form a diamond or rectangular pattern, each piece a serving size, about 3 inches across. Bake at 350 degrees for about 30 minutes, until the top is golden.

2 cups dried apricots
2 cups apple or apricot juice or water
4 eggs

3 cups almonds, toasted and finely chopped
½ cup melted butter
1 pound phyllo dough (*see Appendix*)

1 cup honey

When it has cooled about 20 minutes but is still warm, cut it all the way through the scoring and then drizzle the honey evenly over the entire baklava.

Serve with an apéritif or a cup of your favorite coffee or tea.

Store refrigerated and well covered.

ITALIAN PUDDING

SERVES 6

This smooth, rich, high-protein pudding, studded with multi-colored jewels of fruit, can be dessert, a satisfying salad for luncheon, or a special breakfast.

✣ ✣ ✣

Slice the dried apricots. If you're using unsulfured apricots, soak them in warm water for 20 minutes to plump before slicing.

Using an electric beater or a food processor, whip the ricotta cheese until smooth. Mix in the vanilla and raspberry butter or preserves (make the pudding as sweet as you like by adding more or less). Fold in the fruits and nuts. To insure fluffiness, add the whipped cream not more than two hours before you intend to serve the pudding. Fold in the whipped cream and—voilà!

Serve the pudding in a beautiful bowl and decorate the top with more fruit. We also like Italian Pudding piled on melon wedges for brunch.

¼ cup dried apricots
1 pound ricotta cheese
½ teaspoon pure vanilla extract
¼ to ½ cup raspberry butter or preserves
2 to 3 cups fresh fruit*
¼ cup raisins or dried currants
¼ cup almonds, toasted

1 cup heavy cream, whipped

*The fresh fruit for Italian Pudding may be any combination of blueberries, raspberries, strawberries, grapes, sliced peaches, cubed apples, or cantaloupe. It's a matter of availability and personal choice, but we do not recommend using citrus fruits or pineapple because they may curdle the Italian Pudding.

CHOCOLATE RICOTTA "MOOSE"

SERVES 6

This is one of our most often requested recipes. It makes a foolproof, almost instant, rich and velvety dessert.

Blend the melted chocolate, ricotta cheese, vanilla, and honey in a blender or food processor until very smooth. Pour into dessert cups and chill.

To serve, mound whipped cream on top and garnish with a fresh, ripe strawberry, a few raspberries, an orange or kiwi fruit slice, or shaved chocolate.

3 ounces unsweetened chocolate, melted
1 pound ricotta cheese
1 teaspoon pure vanilla extract
honey to taste (about ⅓ cup)

1 cup heavy cream, whipped with a little vanilla and maple syrup
fresh fruit or shaved chocolate

CREAMY RICE PUDDING

SERVES 6 TO 8

This superb rice pudding has a number of virtues over its cousins: it uses leftover rice, it bakes in the oven, and it's unusually wholesome and delicious. In fact, this dessert may become so popular in your household that you find yourself cooking rice especially to make rice pudding. It's been known to happen.

✤ ✤ ✤

Butter a deep casserole dish and set aside. Preheat the oven to 325 degrees.

In a blender or mixing bowl combine the half-and-half, eggs, vanilla, spices, and honey. In a large bowl thoroughly mix the rice, egg mixture, grated orange peel, raisins, and chopped apples.

Pour the pudding into the casserole dish and bake uncovered for an hour, until the custard is set and the pudding begins to brown lightly at the edges. Stir the pudding thoroughly at 20-minute intervals while it is baking and add a small amount of milk if it becomes too dry.

Serve Creamy Rice Pudding hot from the oven or chill it and serve it cold later. A dollop of fresh whipped cream adds the perfect finishing touch to each serving.

3 cups cooked brown rice (see Appendix)

2¼ cups half-and-half or milk

5 eggs

1 teaspoon pure vanilla extract

½ teaspoon cinnamon

¼ teaspoon ground nutmeg

½ cup honey or maple syrup

2 tablespoons grated orange peel (the peel of one orange)

⅔ cup raisins

2 medium apples, cored and finely chopped (optional)

freshly whipped cream

PIE CRUST

This recipe for an easy-to-handle pastry dough which we use for both dinner and dessert pies is from Tom Walls, our resident pastry-maker, who rolls out the tenderest, flakiest crusts.

✤ ✤ ✤

Sift the flour into a mixing bowl.

Cut the butter into small pieces and sprinkle onto the flour. Working quickly so that the butter will remain cold, use a pastry cutter, two knives, or your fingertips to cut the butter into the flour until the butter pieces are pea-sized.

Sprinkle the ice water over the flour, a little at a time, as you turn the dough with a wooden spoon. As the water is incorporated, a ball of dough will form. Add a little more ice water if the dough fails to come together.

Roll out the dough immediately on a lightly floured board, or chill until firm, 30 to 60 minutes, before rolling.

9-INCH SINGLE PIE CRUST
1 cup unbleached white flour (up to ½ cup whole wheat flour may be substituted)
⅓ cup chilled butter
2 tablespoons ice water
½ teaspoon salt (if unsalted butter is used)

10-INCH SINGLE PIE CRUST
1½ cups unbleached white flour (up to ¾ cups whole wheat flour may be substituted)
½ cup chilled butter
3 tablespoons ice water
½ teaspoon salt (if unsalted butter is used)

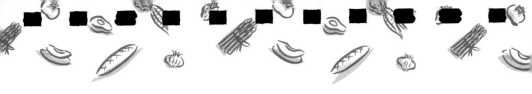

SOUTHERN NUT PIE EUDORA

Our dessert chef, Susan Harville, was excited when she heard that one of her favorite writers, Eudora Welty, was coming to Ithaca to give a reading from her work. Susan made this pie to present to Miss Welty as a token of her appreciation. Miss Welty very graciously accepted the pie and said, " . . . the pleasure you've had from reading my work? Why, surely it couldn't add up to a whole pecan pie!"

Maple syrup, one of our favorite harvests from Ithaca's surrounding hillsides, gives a Northern twist to our version of a Southern classic.

✤ ✤ ✤

Preheat the oven to 375 degrees.

Spread the nuts evenly across the bottom of the unbaked pie shell. Set aside. In a large bowl, mix the melted butter, vanilla, and flour. Add the salt, eggs, maple syrup, and cream and mix thoroughly. Pour the liquid mixture over the nuts in the pie shell. The nuts will float. Push them down into the liquid with the back of a spoon to wet them, so they won't burn during baking.

Bake at 375 degrees for 50 to 60 minutes or until knife inserted in the center comes out clean. Let the pie cool at least 15 minutes before slicing.

Serve plain or with a few crisp apple slices and a dollop of whipped cream or a scoop of ice cream.

1 unbaked 9-inch pie shell (recipe #117)

1½ cups pecan or walnut halves
¼ cup melted butter
1 teaspoon pure vanilla extract
2 tablespoons unbleached white flour
½ teaspoon salt
3 eggs, well beaten
1 cup maple syrup
1 cup heavy cream or half-and-half

apple slices
freshly whipped cream or ice cream

TART LEMON TART

A very tart tart with a cookie crust, this is a refreshing, sophisticated finale for a rich meal, especially welcome on sultry summer evenings. We like to serve this bright lemon tart on a cobalt blue plate.

❖ ❖ ❖

Cut the butter into small pieces and work it into the flour with a pastry cutter, two knives, or your fingertips. Mix in the salt, vanilla, and sugar, and then just enough ice water to bind. Press the dough with your fingers into a 9- or 10-inch drop-bottom tart pan. Chill the crust 1 hour or overnight.

Preheat oven to 425 degrees.

Line the chilled crust with waxed paper and fill with dried beans or rice to prevent the crust from buckling during baking. Bake at 425 degrees for 15 to 20 minutes. Carefully remove the beans and waxed paper.

Lower the oven temperature to 350 degrees.

Mix together the juice of 4 lemons, the butter, and the sugar and heat until the butter melts and the mixture is just warm. Pour the beaten eggs slowly into this mixture in a steady stream, whisking constantly. Continue to stir on low heat until the mixture thickens into a custard. Stir in the vanilla. Pour into the baked crust and bake for 35 to 50 minutes or until the custard sets and the top becomes golden.

Serve chilled and garnished with thinly sliced rounds of lemon.

TART PASTRY
1⅓ cups unbleached white flour
7 tablespoons butter
pinch of salt
¼ teaspoon pure vanilla extract
¼ cup sugar
3 to 4 tablespoons ice water

FILLING
4 lemons
5 tablespoons butter
½ cup sugar
5 eggs, well beaten
¼ teaspoon pure vanilla extract

1 lemon, sliced in very thin rounds

AUNT MINNIE'S FRESH APPLE CAKE

Our Sara Robbins' Aunt Minnie was a renowned Southern cook. This easy-to-make, homey, and moist cake is one reason why.

* * *

Butter a 10-inch bundt pan, two 9-inch round cake pans, or one 9 x 13-inch sheet pan. Sprinkle the bottom and sides of the pan with the sesame seeds.

Preheat the oven to 350 degrees.

Beat the oil and sugar until creamy. Add the eggs one at a time, beating well after each addition. In a separate bowl, sift together the flour, leavenings, and spices. Add the dry ingredients to the egg mixture along with the apple juice and vanilla, beating with a wooden spoon until the batter is smooth. Fold in the chopped apples and nuts.

Pour the batter into the pan and bake for 30 to 45 minutes, depending upon the size of the pan, until a knife inserted in the center comes out clean.

Sprinkle the top with sifted powdered sugar when the cake is cool.

1½ cups vegetable oil
2 cups brown sugar
3 eggs

3 cups sifted flour (half whole wheat pastry flour and half unbleached white flour works well)
1 teaspoon baking soda
1 teaspoon baking powder
¼ teaspoon ground cardamom
1 teaspoon cinnamon

2 teaspoons pure vanilla extract
3 tablespoons apple juice, milk, or water
3 cups chopped apples
1 cup chopped nuts (pecans, walnuts, or almonds)

3 tablespoons sesame seeds
powdered sugar

SPICE CAKE WITH PRUNES AND PECANS

A rich, dark nutty cake that will stay moist almost forever. It's particularly good for the holidays, with all its spices and nuts. With this cake you never know . . . is one slice enough? Are three too many?

✣   ✣   ✣

Preheat the oven to 350 degrees.

Butter and flour a 10-inch bundt pan or a 9 x 13-inch baking pan and set aside.

In a large bowl, beat together the oil, sugar, vanilla, eggs, buttermilk, and prune purée. Sift together the flour, spices, salt, and baking soda and stir these into the wet ingredients. Mix well, then fold in the pecans.

Pour the batter into the pan. Bake for 30 to 45 minutes, depending on the size of the pan, until a knife inserted in the center of the cake comes out clean.

1 cup prune purée*
1 cup vegetable oil
2 cups sugar
1 tablespoon pure vanilla extract
3 eggs, beaten
1 cup buttermilk

2 cups flour (a mixture of unbleached white flour and whole wheat pastry flour is good)
2 teaspoons cinnamon
1 teaspoon ground allspice
1 teaspoon ground cloves
1 teaspoon nutmeg
½ teaspoon salt
1 teaspoon baking soda

1½ cups pecans, chopped

*If not using commercially prepared prune purée, cook 1½ cups of prunes in about ¾ cup of water until soft. Pit the prunes if necessary and purée them in a blender with any remaining cooking water.

MISSISSIPPI MUD CAKE

This is a very dark, moist, adult chocolate cake. It keeps well and travels well. The recipe is from Sarah Begus, a famous Baltimore hostess.

✢ ✢ ✢

Preheat the oven to 275 degrees. (Yes, that really is 275 degrees.)

Generously butter a 10-inch bundt pan and dust it with cocoa.

Sift together the flour, baking soda, and salt. Heat the coffee and liqueur on low heat for about 5 minutes. Add the chocolate and butter and stir until melted. When this mixture is smooth, add the sugar and stir until dissolved. Let the mixture cool for several minutes and then transfer it to a large mixing bowl. Add the flour mixture to the chocolate mixture about a half-cup at a time, beating after each addition until smooth. Then add the eggs and vanilla. Beat for another minute.

Pour the batter into the bundt pan and bake for about 1½ hours, until the cake pulls away from the sides of the pan and springs back when touched in the middle. Remove the cake from the oven and allow to cool for 10 minutes in the pan. Then invert the cake onto a plate. Remove the bundt pan when the cake is completely cool.

This cake is good plain or with whipped cream. Or brush the surface of the cake with 2 or 3 ounces of semi-sweet chocolate, melted and mixed with 1 or 2 tablespoons of cream or coffee.

2 cups unbleached white flour
1 teaspoon baking soda
¼ teaspoon salt

1¾ cups strong freshly brewed coffee
¼ cup bourbon, brandy, or a coffee, chocolate, or mocha liqueur
5 ounces unsweetened chocolate
1 cup butter
2 cups sugar

2 eggs, lightly beaten
1 teaspoon pure vanilla extract

AMARETTO CAKE

If you love the fragrance of almonds, this cake will drive you wild with its heady triple almond whammy–essence, nuts, and liqueur. A cup of cappuccino is the perfect partner.

✢   ✢   ✢

Preheat the oven to 350 degrees.

Generously butter and flour a 10-inch bundt pan and set aside.

Cream together the butter and sugar. The butter should be soft, but not melted. Add the beaten eggs and almond extract and mix well. Blend in two cups of the flour. Combine the milk and ¼ cup of the amaretto and stir into the batter, mixing well. Add the remaining flour and the baking powder, mixing well. Fold in the ground almonds and pour the batter into the bundt pan. Bake for one hour or until a toothpick tests clean.

Cool the cake in the pan for 15 minutes and then pour the remaining ¾ cup of amaretto over the warm cake. Let the amaretto soak in and then invert the cake onto a plate. Remove the pan from the cake when thoroughly cool.

1 pound butter, softened
3 cups sugar
6 eggs, well beaten
2 teaspoons pure almond
   extract
4 cups unbleached white
   flour
¾ cup milk
1 cup amaretto (almond
   liqueur)
2 teaspoons baking
   powder, sifted to
   remove the lumps
2 cups toasted almonds,
   ground

OUR FAVORITE POUND CAKE

Moist, dense, and buttery pound cake is our standard for cake at Moosewood–perfect unadorned, or served with fresh fruit and whipped cream, or frosted, or in a trifle. Once you've mastered the basic cake, try one of our variations and then make up your own.

✢ ✢ ✢

Preheat the oven to 350 degrees.

Generously butter and flour a 10-inch bundt pan and set aside.

Cream the butter and sugar. Beat in the eggs. Add two cups of flour and beat well. Mix in the milk and extract. Combine the baking powder and the remaining 2 cups of flour and then add to the batter. Beat well.

Pour the batter into the bundt pan. Bake about 1 hour, until the cake pulls away from the sides of the pan and a knife inserted in the center comes out clean.

When the cake is done, turn it upside down on a plate to cool, leaving the bundt pan on top of the cake for about 20 minutes, so the cake will hold its shape.

VARIATIONS:
· *Butterscotch Pecan Pound Cake:* Use pure vanilla extract, replace the white sugar with brown sugar, and add 2 cups of toasted pecan halves.

1 pound butter, softened
3 cups sugar
6 eggs
4 cups unbleached white flour
1 cup milk
2 teaspoons pure vanilla, almond, or lemon extract
2 teaspoons baking powder

· *Oasis Cake:* Use apricot juice or coconut milk *(see Appendix)* instead of milk and add ½ cup each of shredded coconut, chopped dried apricots, and chopped dates.

· *Cashew or Peanut Cake:* Use pure vanilla extract, replace half of the butter with cashew butter or peanut butter, and add 1 cup of cashews or toasted peanuts.

· *Cherry-Almond Cake:* Use pure almond extract, reduce the milk to ½ cup, add 1 cup ground toasted almonds with the flour, and at the last minute fold 1½ cups of fresh, pitted whole cherries into the batter. The fruit adds a lot of liquid to the cake during baking, so this batter is stiffer than usual.

· *Whiskey Cake:* Replace all or part of the milk with whiskey.

· *Chocolate Yogurt Pound Cake:* Replace the milk with plain yogurt, reduce the flour to 3½ cups, and add 1 cup cocoa. If you wish, brush melted sweet chocolate on the cooled cake.

· *Marsala Walnut Pound Cake:* Use pure vanilla extract, replace the white sugar with brown sugar, replace the milk with marsala, and add 1 cup chopped toasted walnuts.

· *Layered Pound Cake:* Carefully cut the cooled basic pound cake into 5 layers with a long, serrated bread knife. Spread raspberry butter or conserve between the layers as you rebuild the cake.

GRAPES IN LEMON YOGURT

Grapes in Lemon Yogurt can be served as a salad, dessert, or snack. It's made in seconds and is cool and refreshing. It's especially welcome after a rich or spicy meal. Serve it in stemmed glasses.

- whole seedless white or red grapes
- lemon flavored yogurt (1 cup for each pound of grapes)

* * *

Stir the yogurt into the grapes–they should be coated with yogurt. Serve immediately or chill.

As a salad this dish is a cool accompaniment to Middle Eastern casseroles and stews, such as Moroccan Stew (recipe #62), Kolokithopita (recipe #72), or Zucchini-Feta Casserole (recipe #56).

REFERENCE

RECIPEASEL

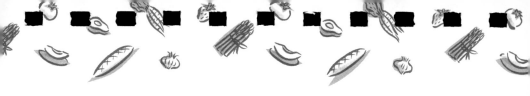

APPENDIX

Many of these ingredients are used in Asian dishes and can be found in Asian food stores and in a growing number of natural food stores.

Annato (Achiote Seed): A hard red seed used in Latin American cooking which imparts a subtle flavor and a beautiful yellow-orange coloring to dishes. Best results are obtained by using the oil in which the seeds have been heated. Place 1 tablespoon whole achiote seeds and 3 to 4 tablespoons vegetable oil in a very small pot or skillet. Maintain a medium heat until the oil turns a bright reddish-orange, approximately 3 to 4 minutes. Strain and discard the seeds. Annato is available in stores that carry foods widely used by the Latin American community.

Artichoke Hearts: Canned artichoke hearts are available in most supermarkets. They are packed in brine or a marinade. When our recipes call for artichoke hearts, use those packed in brine.

Barley: Barley is a sweet, low-starch grain. It requires more water and greater cooking time than most grains.

To Cook: Bring one cup of barley and 5 to 6 cups of water to a boil. Reduce to a simmer and cook about an hour and fifteen minutes. Drain excess water. One cup of raw barley yields 3¾ cups of cooked barley.

Beans: Most dried beans and peas must be softened before they are cooked. No soaking is necessary for lentils or for beans cooked in a pressure cooker. When a recipe calls for cooked beans, canned beans may be substituted; drain and rinse them before using.

Cooking beans: Use the chart below for the correct amount of water and cooking time for specific beans. Before soaking, remove any shriveled or discolored beans and check for pebbles.

Soak the beans by one of these two methods:

1. Add the water to the beans in a saucepan, cover, and soak overnight or for a minimum of 4 hours.

2. Add the water to the beans in a saucepan, cover, and bring to a rapid boil. Remove the pan from the heat and soak for 2 hours.

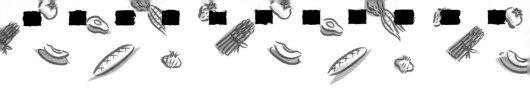

Variety	Water to beans ratio	Cooking time	Cooking equivalent of 1 cup dried
Black turtle beans	4:1	1½ to 2 hours	2 ⅓ cups
Red Kidney beans	3:1	1½ to 2 hours	2 ½ cups
Navy pea beans	3:1	1½ to 2 hours	2 ½ cups
Pinto beans	3:1	1½ to 2 hours	2 ½ cups
Lentils	3:1	1¾ hour	2 cups
Garbanzo beans	2:1	1½ hours	2 ½ cups
Lima beans	2:1	1 hour	2 ½ cups
Split peas	3:1	1 hour	2 cups

After the beans have soaked, drain them, add fresh water, and simmer on medium heat until tender. Check the water level occasionally to avoid scorching. Salt just before serving, or the beans will toughen.

Black Mustard Seeds: These seeds are widely used in Indian cooking, particularly in curries. When added to hot oil, they make a popping sound and release their flavor into the oil. Golden mustard seeds may be substituted but their flavor is somewhat stronger. Black mustard seeds are available in Asian markets and will keep indefinitely in the refrigerator.

Bread Crumbs: We call for bread crumbs in several of our recipes. Bread crumbs are easy to make. Just crush cubes of stale or toasted bread with a rolling pin or whirl them in a blender or food processor. Use a hand grater for chunks of stale bread.

Bread making:

Yeast: One tablespoon of dry yeast equals 1 cake of compressed yeast or 1 package of dry yeast. One package of dry yeast will raise as much as 8 cups of flour. For faster rising, as much as 1 package of dry yeast to each 3 cups of flour may be used. This bread will taste "yeastier." It is important that yeast be fresh. If it isn't fresh and alive, the bread

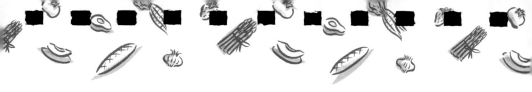

won't rise. Keep yeast refrigerated between bakings. Yeast can also be frozen.

Proofing yeast: To activate dry yeast in preparation for bread making, sprinkle the yeast over warm water. The temperature of the water should be between 100 and 115 degrees, a temperature that feels comfortably warm on the inside of your wrist. Add a little honey or sugar (½ teaspoon) which will nourish the yeast cells as they divide and grow. After about 5 minutes, the yeast should begin to foam. Compressed yeast takes a little longer. If the yeast doesn't foam, it won't raise bread, so start again with new yeast.

Preparing the dough: Add the other liquid ingredients to the proofed yeast and then stir in the flour gradually until the dough is of a consistency that can be kneaded, dry enough that it doesn't stick to your fingers or the bowl.

Gluten: Essential to all yeast breads is the gluten found in wheat flours. Gluten is a protein which makes bread dough strong and elastic. As yeast releases the gases of its respiration, the gluten allows the dough to stretch and form thousands of air-trapping pockets.

Kneading: Kneading the dough distributes the yeast evenly and gives the dough a smooth texture. Knead the dough by pushing the heels of your hands into the dough and then folding it over, occasionally sprinkling more flour on the surface of the dough and the board to prevent sticking. Give the dough a quarter-turn and repeat. Continue repeating this procedure for about 10 minutes. Fully kneaded dough is satiny and should spring back when pressed with a finger.

Rising: Place the dough in a large, buttered bowl and brush the top lightly with oil or melted butter to keep a crust from forming. Cover with a cloth and place in a warm, draft-free spot to rise. Rising times will vary from recipe to recipe. But a general rule is that the dough should be allowed to rise until it doubles in volume which usually takes an hour or two. As a test, make a small indentation in the dough. If the indentation fills back in within a few minutes, allow the dough to continue rising. If the indentation does not disappear, the dough has finished rising. Now comes one of the most satisfying moments in bread making.

Punching down the dough: After punching it down, knead the dough until it is smooth. Form the deflated dough into loaves or rolls

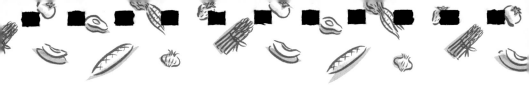

and allow them to rise until almost full-sized. The second rising will take less time than the first. The final fullness will be achieved during baking.

Baking: Bake the loaves for the full time recommended. To test for doneness, tip a loaf out of its baking pan and lightly tap the bottom of the loaf. If the bread is done, there will be a distinctly hollow sound. If it doesn't sound hollow, turn the bread back into the pan and bake a short time longer.

Bulgur: A quick-cooking form of wheat widely used in Balkan and Middle Eastern countries. It is available at natural food stores, Middle Eastern groceries, and often in the international or gourmet food sections of supermarkets. It comes in two textures, fine and coarse.

To cook: Place the bulgur in a bowl with an equal amount of boiling water and a dash of salt. Cover and let sit for 20 to 30 minutes. Stir to fluff. If the bulgur is still too chewy, add another ¼ cup of boiling water, cover, and let sit for 10 minutes more. One cup of dry bulgur yields 2½ cups of cooked bulgur.

Chili Oil: A red oil in which chilies have released their flavor. Chili oil is used as a spice in Asian cooking–sparingly! Available

at Asian food stores, chili oil is also easily made at home. Just heat 1 cup of peanut or vegetable oil until hot but not smoking. Stir in about 2 dozen small dried red chilies, 3 tablespoons red pepper flakes, or 1 tablespoon cayenne. Cover, cool, and strain.

Chili Paste with Garlic, or Szechuan Chili Paste: A spicy condiment made with chili peppers, salt, and garlic. It will keep almost indefinitely when refrigerated.

Chinese Fermented Black Beans: These are preserved black soybeans with a pungent, salty taste, used as a seasoning rather than as a main ingredient. Generally they are either rinsed under running water or soaked for a short time in water to soften them and remove some of their saltiness before being used in cooking.

Chinese Rice Wine or Shaoxing: A traditional Chinese cooking wine named for its place of origin. Shaoxing is similar to a dry sherry, but cooking sherry, which is sweet, should not be substituted.

Coconut Milk: Coconut milk is used in Southeast Asian and Pacific cuisines in sauces, soups, curries, and desserts. The coconut "milk" or "mix" which is intended for use in mixed drinks is very sweet and

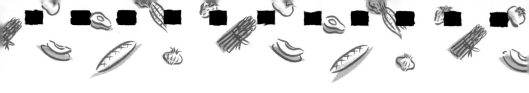

different and should not be used as a substitute.

Couscous: A staple food of North Africa, couscous is finely milled semolina wheat, essentially tiny pearls of pasta. We use the quick-cooking variety. Couscous is available in Middle Eastern, Greek, and natural food stores and in the international foods sections of supermarkets.

Steeping couscous: Place equal amounts of dry couscous and boiling water with a little salt and butter or oil in a bowl. Cover and let sit 10 to 15 minutes, stirring frequently to fluff. If it is still crunchy, add another ¼ cup of boiling water, stir, cover, and let sit another 5 minutes.

Steaming couscous: Place the couscous in a fine-meshed sieve or a colander lined with cheesecloth. Rest the sieve on the rim of a deep pot so that the bottom of the sieve is a couple inches above the pot bottom. Pour several cups of boiling water over the couscous, making sure to dampen all of the grains. Using foil, tightly cover the pot to seal in the steam. After 5 minutes, stir the couscous to fluff. If the couscous is still crunchy, pour in some more boiling water, taking care that the water doesn't reach high

enough to touch the sieve. Cover the pot again and check the couscous after 5 minutes. Stir to fluff when the couscous is ready. Place it in a serving bowl and stir in salt to taste and some butter or a little oil. Use the steaming method to reheat leftover couscous.

Croutons: Croutons are easily made from bread past its peak of freshness. Cube the bread. Spread the cubes on a baking sheet and place in a preheated 350 degree oven, stirring occasionally, until crispy, about 10 to 15 minutes. Meanwhile melt some butter. Sauté minced or pressed garlic in the butter until it is golden. Add a pinch of herbs, such as thyme, summer savory, oregano, or marjoram. Toss the bread cubes and garlic-butter well in a bowl. Serve croutons warm or at room temperature. Croutons will keep up to 2 weeks in an airtight container.

Curry Powder: Curry powders bought in spice shops or Indian food stores vary greatly in flavor, aroma, and "hotness." Curry powder may be mixed at home. At Moosewood we use a small coffee grinder to grind whole curry spices. The following is a suggestion for mixing curry powder; experiment to find a combination you find pleasing:

2 teaspoons ground cumin
2 teaspoons ground coriander
2 teaspoons turmeric
½ teaspoon ground cinnamon
¼ teaspoon ground nutmeg
¼ teaspoon ground cayenne pepper
¼ teaspoon ground black pepper
¼ teaspoon ground cloves
¼ teaspoon ground cardamom

Unless you've roasted the spices before grinding, curry powder should be cooked briefly in a little butter or oil to bring out its full flavor before it is added to foods.

Egg Whites: To beat egg whites, separate the whites from the yolks by cracking the egg over a bowl and gently breaking in two, keeping the yolk in one half of the shell. Let the white drain off into the bowl by slipping the yolk from one half shell to the other. Using either an electric mixer or a whisk, beat the whites at a steady, high speed. A pinch of salt or cream of tartar will hurry the process along. The whites are stiff when peaks form that will stand by themselves.

Fish Sauce: Fish sauce is an extract of fermented fish which is used as a basic flavoring in the cuisines of Thailand, Vietnam, the Philippines, and China. It has a distinctive flavor and an odor which disappears when the fish sauce is cooked.

Hungarian Paprika: To insure retaining the delicate flavor of this spice, avoid scorching. Hot paprika can be used in place of cayenne.

Leeks: To prepare leeks, cut off the roots and tops, leaving 8 to 10 inches of bulb and lower leaf. The tops of the leek leaves are tough and should be discarded or used in stock. Leeks are grown in sandy soil and should be washed carefully. Slice the leek down the middle almost to the root and, holding it under running water or immersed in a basin of water, pull each layer away from the bulb, rinsing well. Drain or shake dry. Slice or chop according to recipe directions.

Lemon Grass: A citrus-flavored herb used in Southeast Asian cooking. Grind dried lemon grass to a powder before using. Once it's ground, it quickly loses its flavor. Grated lemon peel, substituted in the same quantity, provides piquancy but a different flavor.

Matzoh: Square, unleavened wheat crackers available in the kosher food section of the supermarket. Finely ground matzoh is referred to as matzoh meal and is used in Jewish cooking in place of bread crumbs.

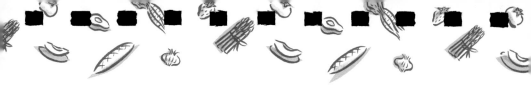

Mirin: A golden, sweet cooking wine made from sake, sweet rice, and rice malt. Mirin's alcohol content evaporates in the cooking process, leaving a subtle and unique sweetness. If mirin is not available, substitute sugar or another sweetener in one-third the amount of mirin called for.

Miso: Miso imparts a rich, full flavor to food. It ranges in color from dark brown to light. In the United States the three best known varieties of miso are rice miso, barley miso, and soy miso. Rice miso, also called light miso, is yellow to amber in color and relatively sweet. Barley miso, also called red miso, is darker colored and very savory. Soy miso is usually thickest and strongest in flavor. We primarily use a miso called Onozaki, an unpasteurized rice miso made by the Onozaki family on their farm in Japan. We use it in soups, stews, spreads, and salad dressing. Miso should not be boiled. Boiling destroys the digestion-aiding enzymes created in the fermentation process.

Nori: Also called laver. Dark green or purplish seaweed sold dried in thin sheets packaged in cellophane or in cans and available in gourmet or Asian food stores. Nori is used to wrap filling or, crumbled, as a seasoning. The flavor of nori is enhanced if you "toast" it just before use by very briefly passing it over a gas flame until it becomes greenish and crisp. It is best stored tightly wrapped and frozen.

Phyllo Pastry Dough: Also spelled filo. These very thin sheets of dough are used to make flaky, crispy pastries and strudels. Packaged phyllo dough is available refrigerated or frozen in many supermarkets and in Mediterranean or Middle Eastern food stores.

Polenta: A staple of Northern Italian cooking, this is a cereal made from cornmeal and water, and often enriched with butter and grated cheese. It is also good cooked according to the directions below, poured into a buttered baking dish to about 1 inch deep to cool, and then cut into squares and fried.

To cook: For each cup of cornmeal, use 3 cups of water. Use a heavy pot or a "waffle" (see Waffle) during the simmer to prevent from sticking. Bring the water to a boil. Sprinkle in the cornmeal while whisking briskly. Simmer on low heat about 20 minutes, stirring occasionally. Stir in salt and butter and/or cheese to taste.

Potato Flour: A very fine flour made from cooked, dried, and ground potatoes. Potato

flour makes a good coating for crispy, deep-fried tofu. It can often be found in the kosher food sections of supermarkets.

Purée: This process is most easily done in a blender or food processor but can also be accomplished with a sieve. When using a blender or food processor, whirl the vegetables, beans, fruit, etc., with a liquid until smooth. If a sieve is used, place the cooked food in the sieve over a bowl or pot and push it through the mesh with the back of a large spoon or potato masher. Mix in the liquid last.

Rice:

To cook: A heavy saucepan or pot with a tight-fitting lid is best for cooking rice, because it retains more moisture and is less apt to scorch the rice. Good rice can be made in a lighter pot with the same use of a flame spreader or "waffle" (see Waffle).

When uncooked rice is sautéed briefly in oil before the water is added, it yields non-gummy, clearly separated grains of cooked rice. Before adding the water, sauté the rice in a little oil for a minute or two, stirring briskly. We've learned a foolproof way to determine a good water-to-rice ratio from the Southeast Asians. After the rice has been measured into the pot (but before it has been sautéed) push your index finger through the rice to the bottom of the pot and note, or mark with your thumbnail, how far up your finger the rice reaches. Sauté the rice and turn off the heat. Then touch the top of the rice with the tip of your finger and add cool water to the pot until it meets that point on your finger where the rice originally reached. The depth of the water (from the bottom of the pot to the surface of the water) should be double the depth of the rice alone, unless the rice is deeper than one inch. In that case be sure that you have no more than one inch of water above the level of the rice.

Add a pinch of salt, if you wish. Cover the pot and bring the rice to a boil. When you see steam escaping from the lid, turn the heat off for 5 minutes and then simmer the rice on very low heat for 25 minutes. Use a "waffle" at this point if your pot is light or if the heat won't go very low. Honor another time-tested Asian practice: resist looking into the rice once it has come to a boil. Rice is always better steamed, and lifting the lid will spoil that.

After the simmer, let the rice stand off the heat for 10 minutes, then stir it well.

Rice Vinegar: There are many varieties of vinegar made from different rice wines. For use in recipes in this recipeasel, buy a clear or golden variety, either Chinese or Japanese. Avoid brands that contain added sugar, salt, or monosodium glutamate (MSG).

Roux: A mixture of butter or oil and flour used to thicken sauces, soups, and stews. Sprinkle flour into the melted, bubbling butter, whisking constantly to make a smooth paste. Simmer for a few minutes. Slowly pour heated liquid into the roux, whisking or stirring vigorously until it thickens. Using hot liquid speeds up the thickening.

Scalded Milk: Milk that has been heated to just below the boiling point.

Sesame Oil: Thick, amber-colored, and wonderfully aromatic, this oil is made from roasted sesame seeds. We specify "dark" sesame oil so it will not be confused with paler cold-pressed sesame oil. "Dark" sesame oil is used for seasoning, not for cooking. It burns easily and loses its distinctive, nutty flavor when overheated.

Shiitake Mushrooms: They are expensive– but a very few will richly flavor a dish. To soften the dried mushrooms, submerge in boiling water, cover, and soak for at least an hour. After soaking, cut the caps from the stems, slice caps thinly, and add to sautés, stews, or soups. The soaking liquid is an excellent addition to stocks or sauces.

Soba: Widely known as "Japanese pasta," these noodles are brownish-gray, usually flat and thin, and they vary in texture and density. Soba are used traditionally in miso broths but adapt well to chilled, Asian pasta salads.

Soy Flour: Made from ground soy beans. Used primarily in bread baking to boost the protein content.

Star Anise: A strong-flavored, aromatic spice used in Chinese and Southeast Asian cooking. Star anise comes from brown pods in 8-pointed star-shaped clusters. To use, break off "points" (1 or 2 are usually ample) from the whole cluster and tie in cheesecloth or place in a "spice bob" to simmer in the cooking food. Chinese Five Spice Powder, which is sold in Asian food stores, has star anise as an ingredient and is the only substitute we know for star anise that will give a similar flavor.

Strudel: Assembling strudel is simple. First melt a quarter-pound of butter. Using a pastry brush, butter the baking sheet. Unfold phyllo leaves. To make a basic rectangle, count out 6

to 8 leaves from the corner of the stack. Lift them up and lay them flat on the baking sheet. Spread the filling over the middle of the leaves, leaving 3-inch edges all around. Brush the edges with butter. For the top, lay down two leaves at a time, buttering the top leaf each time. After 4 or 5 pairs, fold the corners of all the phyllo leaves up over the filling, butter, then neatly fold each side up over the filling and butter. Lay down two more pairs of leaves, buttering the top leaf of each pair. Then tuck the new edges under the strudel, corners first, then sides. Bake 45 minutes to an hour.

Szechuan Peppercorns: Nutty, spicy, small, reddish-brown peppercorns used in Chinese cooking. Briefly toast peppercorns in a hot skillet until they begin to smoke. Remove and pulverize in a spice grinder or with a mortar and pestle.

Tahini: Tahini is not to be confused with sesame butter, which is denser, stronger-tasting. Tahini is widely used in Middle Eastern cooking and is usually available in natural food stores and Middle Eastern and Greek groceries.

Tamari Soy Sauce: Although the terms "soy sauce" and "tamari" are often used inter-changeably, tamari, a by-product of the miso-making process, is an entirely different product. It is stronger in taste and must be used with care as a replacement for soy sauce. It is also wheat-free, a blessing for the allergic.

Tamarind: Tamarind pulp is sold in concentrated form in jars or dried in brick form. The pods are also available. Dried tamarind must be softened before use: break off a piece, pour boiling water over it, and let it sit for about 30 minutes until soft. Mash and then strain out the seeds and fibers. Tamarind is acidic and is used much like lemon juice. Although lemon juice has a different flavor, it can be substituted for tamarind at a ratio of 2 to 1. Tamarind is available in Indian and Asian food stores.

Tempeh: Tempeh is made from cultured soybeans. If you're lucky, you'll find it fresh in your area, but it is available frozen in most natural food stores. Thaw tempeh before using in a recipe. Slice or cube tempeh when it is partially thawed to avoid the crumbling which sometimes occurs when slicing fully thawed tempeh.

Tofu: Tofu is fresh soybean curd, a highly versatile and protein-rich food. Commercial

cakes of tofu vary in size and firmness, making it difficult to describe exact amounts in recipes, but generally smaller cakes of tofu are also firmer and so about equivalent to the larger, softer cakes. We use 12-ounce cakes of medium-soft tofu.

To press tofu: Most recipes call for pressed tofu because pressing makes the tofu firmer and more absorbent. To press tofu, place the cakes of tofu between two flat plates or baking sheets. Weight the top with a bowl of water, a stack of plates, a heavy can, or whatever is handy. The sides of the cakes of tofu should bulge out a little, but not split. Let stand for at least 30 minutes, remove the press, and pour off the water.

To blanch tofu: When using tofu uncooked (marinated, mashed, puréed, etc.), blanch it after pressing and before going on with the recipe. To blanch tofu, drop whole cakes or cubed tofu into boiling water. Simmer for about 5 minutes and remove from the water. Blanching firms tofu, keeps it from diluting what it is added to, and makes it more absorbent.

Tofu Kan: Tofu kan is firmly pressed tofu baked or simmered with spices, soy sauce, and barley malt syrup. Five-spice tofu can be substituted for tofu kan in equal quantity.

Waffle: Also known as "flame spreader" or "flame tamer," a waffle is a round metal plate that sits between the burner and cooking pot. It serves to reduce the heat and to distribute the heat evenly. Waffles can be purchased at restaurant or kitchen supply stores.

Wakame: A mild-tasting seaweed especially rich in iodine. Dried wakame should be soaked for 15 minutes in water to soften it and to remove excess salt. Discard the water, cut out the midrib, and chop it into small pieces.

Wasabi: A green Japanese radish with the assertive flavor and sinus-clearing effect you may have enjoyed in sushi. Mix the powder with water to form a smooth paste, cover, and set aside a few minutes while the flavor develops fully. Wasabi is very pungent and should be used very sparingly.

INDEX

YOUR RECIPE NAME:

INGREDIENTS:

INSTRUCTIONS:

YOUR RECIPE NAME:

INSTRUCTIONS:

INGREDIENTS:

YOUR RECIPE NAME:

INGREDIENTS:

INSTRUCTIONS:

YOUR RECIPE NAME:

INSTRUCTIONS:

INGREDIENTS:

YOUR RECIPE NAME:

INGREDIENTS:

INSTRUCTIONS: